THE THEORY OF SOCIAL
REVOLUTIONS

THE MACMILLAN COMPANY
NEW YORK · BOSTON · CHICAGO · DALLAS
ATLANTA · SAN FRANCISCO

MACMILLAN & CO., Limited
LONDON · BOMBAY · CALCUTTA
MELBOURNE

THE MACMILLAN CO. OF CANADA, Ltd.
TORONTO

THE THEORY OF SOCIAL REVOLUTIONS

BY

BROOKS ADAMS

New York
THE MACMILLAN COMPANY
1913

All rights reserved

COPYRIGHT, 1913,
BY THE ATLANTIC MONTHLY COMPANY.

COPYRIGHT, 1913,
BY THE MACMILLAN COMPANY.

Set up and electrotyped. Published September, 1913.

Norwood Press
J. S. Cushing Co. — Berwick & Smith Co.
Norwood, Mass., U.S.A.

PREFATORY NOTE

THE first chapter of the following book was published, in substantially its present form, in the *Atlantic Monthly* for April, 1913. I have to thank the editor for his courtesy in assenting to my wish to reprint. The other chapters have not appeared before. I desire also to express my obligations to my learned friend, Dr. M. M. Bigelow, who, most kindly, at my request, read chapters two and three, which deal with the constitutional law, and gave me the benefit of his most valuable criticism.

Further than this I have but one word to add. I have written in support of no political movement, nor for any ephemeral purpose. I have written only to express a deep conviction which is the result of more than twenty years of study, and reflection upon this subject.

BROOKS ADAMS.

QUINCY, MASSACHUSETTS,
   May 17, 1913.

CONTENTS

CHAPTER		PAGE
I.	THE COLLAPSE OF CAPITALISTIC GOVERNMENT	1
II.	THE LIMITATIONS OF THE JUDICIAL FUNCTION	36
III.	AMERICAN COURTS AS LEGISLATIVE CHAMBERS	80
IV.	THE SOCIAL EQUILIBRIUM	132
V.	POLITICAL COURTS	160
VI.	INFERENCES	203
INDEX		231

THE THEORY OF SOCIAL REVOLUTIONS

CHAPTER I

THE COLLAPSE OF CAPITALISTIC GOVERNMENT

CIVILIZATION, I apprehend, is nearly synonymous with order. However much we may differ touching such matters as the distribution of property, the domestic relations, the law of inheritance and the like, most of us, I should suppose, would agree that without order civilization, as we understand it, cannot exist. Now, although the optimist contends that, since man cannot foresee the future, worry about the future is futile, and that everything, in the best possible of worlds, is inevitably for the best, I think it clear that within recent years an uneasy suspicion has come into being that the principle of authority has been dangerously impaired, and that the social system, if it is to cohere, must be reorganized. So far as my observation has extended, such intuitions are usually not without an adequate cause, and if there be reason for anxiety anywhere, it surely should be in the United States, with its unwieldy bulk, its heterogeneous population, and its complex government. Therefore, I submit, that an hour may not be quite wasted which is passed in considering some of the recent phenomena which have appeared about us, in order to ascertain if they can be grouped together in any comprehensible relation.

About a century ago, after the American and French Revolutions and the Napoleonic wars, the present industrial era opened, and brought with it a new governing class, as every considerable change in human environment must bring with it a governing class to give it expression. Perhaps, for lack of a recognized name, I may describe this class as the industrial capitalistic class, composed in the main of administrators and bankers. As nothing in the universe is stationary, ruling classes have their rise, culmination, and decline, and I conjecture that this class attained to its acme of popularity and power, at least in America, toward the close of the third quarter of the nineteenth century. I draw this inference from the fact that in the next quarter resistance to capitalistic methods began to take shape in such legislation as the Interstate Commerce Law and the Sherman Act, and almost at the opening of the present century a progressively rigorous opposition found for its mouthpiece the President of the Union himself. History may not be a very practical study, but it teaches some useful lessons, one of which is that nothing is accidental, and that if men move in a given direction, they do so in obedience to an impulsion as automatic as is the impulsion of gravitation. Therefore, if Mr. Roosevelt became, what his adversaries are pleased to call, an agitator, his agitation had a cause which is as deserving of study as is the path of a cyclone. This problem has long interested me, and I harbor no doubt not only that the equilibrium of society is very rapidly shifting, but that Mr. Roosevelt has, half-automatically, been stimulated by the instability about him to seek for a new centre of social gravity. In plain English, I infer that he has concluded that industrialism has induced conditions which can no longer be controlled by the old capitalistic methods, and that the country must be brought to a level of administrative efficiency competent to deal with the strains and stresses of the twentieth century, just as, a hundred and twenty-five years ago, the country was brought to an administrative level competent for that age, by the adoption of the Constitution. Acting on these premises, as I conjecture, whether consciously worked out or not, Mr. Roosevelt's next step was to begin the readjustment; but, I infer, that on attempting any correlated measures of reform, Mr. Roosevelt found progress impossible, because of the obstruction of the courts. Hence his instinct led him to try to overleap that obstruction, and he suggested, without, I suspect, examining the problem very deeply, that the people should assume the right of "recalling" judicial decisions made in causes which involved the nullifying of legislation. What would have happened had Mr. Roosevelt been given the opportunity to thoroughly formulate his ideas, even in the midst of an election, can never be known, for it chanced that he was forced to deal with subjects as vast and complex as ever vexed a statesman or a jurist, under difficulties at least equal to the difficulties of the task itself.

If the modern mind has developed one characteristic more markedly than another, it is an impatience with prolonged demands on its attention, especially if the subject be tedious. No one could imagine that the New York press of to-day would print the disquisitions which Hamilton wrote in 1788 in support of the Constitution, or that, if it did, any one would read them, least of all the lawyers; and yet Mr. Roosevelt's audience was emotional and discursive even for a modern American audience. Hence, if he attempted to lead at all, he had little choice but to adopt, or at least discuss, every nostrum for reaching an immediate millennium which happened to be uppermost; although, at the same time, he had to defend himself against an attack compared with which any criticism to which Hamilton may have been subjected resembled a caress. The result has been that the Progressive movement, bearing Mr. Roosevelt with it, has degenerated into a disintegrating rather than a constructive energy, which is, I suspect, likely to become a danger to every one interested in the maintenance of order, not to say in the stability of property. Mr Roosevelt is admittedly a strong and determined man whose instinct is arbitrary, and yet, if my analysis be sound, we see him, at the supreme moment of his life, diverted from his chosen path toward centralization of power, and projected into an environment of, apparently, for the most part, philanthropists and women, who could hardly conceivably form a party fit to aid him in establishing a vigorous, consolidated, administrative system. He must have found the pressure toward disintegration resistless, and if we consider this most significant phenomenon, in connection with an abundance of similar phenomena, in other countries, which indicate social incoherence, we can hardly resist a growing apprehension touching the future. Nor is that apprehension allayed if, to reassure ourselves, we turn to history, for there we find on every side long series of precedents more ominous still.

Were all other evidence lacking, the inference that radical changes are at hand might be deduced from the past. In the experience of the English-speaking race, about once in every three generations a social convulsion has occurred; and probably such catastrophes must continue to occur in order that laws and institutions may be adapted to physical growth. Human society is a living organism, working mechanically, like any other organism. It has members, a circulation, a nervous system, and a sort of skin or envelope, consisting of its laws and institutions. This skin, or envelope, however, does not expand automatically, as it would had Providence intended humanity to be peaceful, but is only fitted to new conditions by those painful and conscious efforts which we call revolutions. Usually these revolutions are warlike, but sometimes they are benign, as was the revolution over which General Washington, our first great " Progressive," presided, when the rotting Confederation, under his guidance, was converted into a relatively excellent administrative system by the adoption of the Constitution.

Taken for all in all, I conceive General Washington to have been the greatest man of the eighteenth century, but to me his greatness chiefly consists in that balance of mind which enabled him to recognize when an old order had passed away, and to perceive how a new order could be best introduced. Joseph Story was ten years old in 1789 when the Constitution was adopted; his earliest impressions, therefore, were of the Confederation, and I know no better description of the interval just subsequent to the peace of 1783, than is contained in a few lines in his dissenting opinion in the Charles River Bridge Case: —

"In order to entertain a just view of this subject, we must go back to that period of general bankruptcy, and distress and difficulty (1785). . . . The union of the States was crumbling into ruins, under the old Confederation. Agriculture, manufactures, and commerce were at their lowest ebb. There was infinite danger to all the States from local interests and jealousies, and from the apparent impossibility of a much longer adherence to that shadow of a government, the Continental Congress. And even four years afterwards, when every evil had been greatly aggravated, and civil war was added to other calamities, the Constitution of the United States was all but shipwrecked in passing through the state conventions."[1]

This crisis, according to my computation, was the normal one of the third generation. Between 1688 and 1765 the British Empire had physically outgrown its legal envelope, and the consequence was a revolution. The thirteen American colonies, which formed the western section of the imperial

[1] Charles River Bridge v. Warren Bridge, 11 Peters, 608, 609.

mass, split from the core and drifted into chaos, beyond the constraint of existing law. Washington was, in his way, a large capitalist, but he was much more. He was not only a wealthy planter, but he was an engineer, a traveller, to an extent a manufacturer, a politician, and a soldier, and he saw that, as a conservative, he must be " Progressive" and raise the law to a power high enough to constrain all these thirteen refractory units. For Washington understood that peace does not consist in talking platitudes at conferences, but in organizing a sovereignty strong enough to coerce its subjects.

The problem of constructing such a sovereignty was the problem which Washington solved, temporarily at least, without violence. He prevailed not only because of an intelligence and elevation of character which enabled him to comprehend, and to persuade others, that, to attain a common end, all must make sacrifices, but also because he was supported by a body of the most remarkable men whom America has ever produced. Men who, though doubtless in a numerical minority, taking the country as a whole, by sheer weight of ability and energy, achieved their purpose.

Yet even Washington and his adherents could not alter the limitations of the human mind. He could postpone, but he could not avert, the impact of conflicting social forces. In 1789 he compromised, but he did not determine the question of sovereignty. He eluded an impending conflict by introducing courts as political arbitrators, and the expedient worked more or less well until the tension reached a certain point. Then it broke down, and the question of sovereignty had to be settled in America, as elsewhere, on the field of battle. It was not decided until Appomattox. But the function of the courts in American life is a subject which I shall consider hereafter.

If the invention of gunpowder and printing in the fourteenth and fifteenth centuries presaged the Reformation of the sixteenth, and if the Industrial Revolution of the eighteenth was the forerunner of political revolutions throughout the Western World, we may well, after the mechanical and economic cataclysm of the nineteenth, cease wondering that twentieth-century society should be radical.

Never since man first walked erect have his relations toward nature been so changed, within the same space of time, as they have been since Washington was elected President and the Parisian mob stormed the Bastille. Washington found the task of a readjustment heavy enough, but the civilization he knew was simple. When Washington lived, the fund of energy at man's disposal had not very sensibly augmented since the fall of Rome. In the eighteenth, as in the fourth century, engineers had at command only animal power, and a little wind and water power, to which had been added, at the end of the Middle Ages, a low explosive. There was nothing in the daily life of his age which made the legal and administrative principles which had sufficed for Justinian insufficient for him. Twentieth-century society rests on a basis not different so much in degree, as in kind, from all that has gone before. Through applied science infinite forces have been domesticated, and the action of these infinite forces upon finite minds has been to create a tension, together with a social acceleration and concentration, not only unparalleled, but, apparently, without limit. Meanwhile our laws and institutions have remained, in substance, constant. I doubt if we have developed a single important administrative principle which would be novel to Napoleon, were he to live again, and I am quite sure that we have no legal principle younger than Justinian.

As a result, society has been squeezed, as it were, from its rigid eighteenth-century legal shell, and has passed into a fourth dimension of space, where it performs its most important functions beyond the cognizance of the law, which remains in a space of but three dimensions. Washington encountered a somewhat analogous problem when dealing with the thirteen petty independent states, which had escaped from England; but his problem was relatively rudimentary. Taking the theory of sovereignty as it stood, he had only to apply it to communities. It was mainly a question of concentrating a sufficient amount of energy to enforce order in sovereign social units. The whole social detail remained unchanged. Our conditions would seem to imply a very considerable extension and specialization of the principle of sovereignty, together with a commensurate increment of energy, but unfortunately the twentieth-century American problem is still further complicated by the character of the envelope in which this highly volatilized society is theoretically contained. To attain his object, Washington introduced a written organic law, which of all things is the most inflexible. No other modern nation has to consider such an impediment.

Moneyed capital I take to be stored human energy, as a coal measure is stored solar energy; and moneyed capital, under the stress of modern life, has developed at once extreme fluidity, and an equivalent compressibility. Thus a small number of men can control it in enormous masses, and so it comes to pass that, in a community like the United States, a few men, or even, in certain emergencies, a single man, may become clothed with various of the attributes of sovereignty. Sovereign powers are powers so important that the community, in its corporate capacity, has, as society has centralized, usually found it necessary to monopolize them more or less absolutely, since their possession by private persons causes revolt. These powers, when vested in some official, as, for example, a king or emperor, have been held by him, in all Western countries at least, as a trust to be used for the common welfare. A breach of that trust has commonly been punished by deposition or death. It was upon a charge of breach of trust that Charles I, among other sovereigns, was tried and executed. In short, the relation of sovereign and subject has been based either upon consent and mutual obligation, or upon submission to a divine command; but, in either case, upon recognition of responsibility. Only the relation of master and slave implies the status of sovereign power vested in an unaccountable superior. Nevertheless, it is in a relation somewhat analogous to the latter, that the modern capitalist has been placed toward his fellow citizens, by the advances in applied science. An example or two will explain my meaning.

High among sovereign powers has always ranked the ownership and administration of highways. And it is evident why this should have been so. Movement is life, and the stoppage of movement is death, and the movement of every people flows along its highways. An invader has only to cut the communications of the invaded to paralyze him, as he would paralyze an animal by cutting his arteries or tendons. Accordingly, in all ages and in all lands, down to the nineteenth century, nations even partially centralized have, in their corporate capacity, owned and cared for their highways, either directly or through accountable agents. And they have paid for them by direct taxes, like the Romans, or by tolls levied upon traffic, as many mediæval governments preferred to do. Either method answers its purpose, provided the government recognizes its responsibility; and no government ever recognized this responsibility more fully than did the autocratic government of ancient Rome. So the absolute régime of eighteenth-century France recognized this responsibility when Louis XVI undertook to remedy the abuse of unequal taxation, for the maintenance of the highways, by abolishing the corvée.

Toward the middle of the nineteenth century, the application, by science, of steam to locomotion, made railways a favorite speculation. Forthwith, private capital acquired these highways, and because of the inelasticity of the old law, treated them as ordinary chattels, to be administered for the profit of the owner exclusively. It is true that railway companies posed as public agents when demanding the power to take private property; but when it came to charging for use of their ways, they claimed to be only private carriers, authorized to bargain as they pleased. Indeed, it grew to be considered a mark of efficient railroad management to extract the largest revenue possible from the people, along the lines of least resistance; that is, by taxing most heavily those individuals and localities which could least resist. And the claim by the railroads that they might do this as a matter of right was long upheld by the courts,[1] nor have the judges even yet, after a generation of revolt and of legislation, altogether abandoned this doctrine.

The courts — reluctantly, it is true, and principally at the instigation of the railways themselves, who found the practice unprofitable — have latterly discountenanced discrimination as to persons, but they still uphold discrimination as to localities.[2] Now, among abuses of sovereign power, this is one of the most galling, for of all taxes the transportation tax is perhaps that

[1] Fitchburg R. R. v. Gage, 12 Gray 393, and innumerable cases following it.

[2] See the decisions of the Commerce Court on the Long and Short-Haul Clause. Atchison, T. & S. F. Ry. v. United States, 191 Federal Rep. 856.

which is most searching, most insidious, and, when misused, most destructive. The price paid for transportation is not so essential to the public welfare as its equality; for neither persons nor localities can prosper when the necessaries of life cost them more than they cost their competitors. In towns, no cup of water can be drunk, no crust of bread eaten, no garment worn, which has not paid the transportation tax, and the farmer's crops must rot upon his land, if other farmers pay enough less than he to exclude him from markets toward which they all stand in a position otherwise equal. Yet this formidable power has been usurped by private persons who have used it purely selfishly, as no legitimate sovereign could have used it, and by persons who have indignantly denounced all attempts to hold them accountable, as an infringement of their constitutional rights. Obviously, capital cannot assume the position of an irresponsible sovereign, living in a sphere beyond the domain of law, without inviting the fate which has awaited all sovereigns who have denied or abused their trust.

The operation of the New York Clearing-House is another example of the acquisition of sovereign power by irresponsible private persons. Primarily, of course, a clearing-house is an innocent institution occupied with adjusting balances between banks, and has no relation to the volume of the currency. Furthermore, among all highly centralized nations, the regulation of the currency is one of the most jealously guarded of the prerogatives of sovereignty, because all values hinge upon the relation which the volume of the currency bears to the volume of trade. Yet, as everybody knows, in moments of financial panic, the handful of financiers who, directly or indirectly, govern the Clearing-House, have it in their power either to expand or to contract the currency, by issuing or by withdrawing Clearing-House certificates, more effectually perhaps than if they controlled the Treasury of the United States. Nor does this power, vast as it is, at all represent the supremacy which a few bankers enjoy over values, because of their facilities for manipulating the currency and, with the currency, credit; facilities, which are used or abused entirely beyond the reach of the law.

Bankers, at their conventions and through the press, are wont to denounce the American monetary system, and without doubt all that they say, and much more that they do not say, is true; and yet I should suppose that there could be little doubt that American financiers might, after the panic of 1893, and before the administration of Mr. Taft, have obtained from Congress, at most sessions, very reasonable legislation, had they first agreed upon the reforms they demanded, and, secondly, manifested their readiness, as a condition precedent to such reforms, to submit to effective government supervision in those departments of their business which relate to the inflation or depression of values. They have shown little inclination to submit to restraint in these particulars, nor, perhaps, is their reluctance surprising, for the possession by a very small favored class of the unquestioned privilege, whether actually used or not, at recurring intervals, of subjecting the debtor class to such pressure as the creditor may think necessary, in order to force the debtor to surrender his property to the creditor at the creditor's price, is a wonder beside which Aladdin's lamp burns dim.

As I have already remarked, I apprehend that sovereignty is a variable quantity of administrative energy, which, in civilizations which we call advancing, tends to accumulate with a rapidity proportionate to the acceleration of movement. That is to say, the community, as it consolidates, finds it essential to its safety to withdraw, more or less completely, from individuals, and to monopolize, more or less strictly, itself, a great variety of functions. At one stage of civilization the head of the family administers justice, maintains an armed force for war or police, wages war, makes treaties of peace, coins money, and, not infrequently, wears a crown, usually of a form to indicate his importance in a hierarchy. At a later stage of civilization, companies of traders play a great part. Such aggregations of private and irresponsible adventurers have invaded and conquered empires, founded colonies, and administered justice to millions of human beings. In our own time, we have seen the assumption of many of the functions of these and similar private companies by the sovereign. We have seen the East India Company absorbed by the British Parliament; we have seen the railways, and the telephone and the telegraph companies, taken into possession, very generally, by the most progressive governments of the world; and now we have come to the necessity of dealing with the domestic-trade monopoly, because trade has fallen into monopoly through the centralization of capital in a constantly contracting circle of ownership.

Among innumerable kinds of monopolies none have been more troublesome than trade monopolies, especially those which control the price of the necessaries of life; for, so far as I know, no people, approximately free, have long endured such monopolies patiently. Nor could they well have done so without constraint by overpowering physical force, for the possession of a monopoly of a necessary of life by an individual, or by a small privileged class, is tantamount to investing a minority, contemptible alike in numbers and in physical force, with an arbitrary and unlimited power to tax the majority, not for public, but for private purposes. Therefore it has not infrequently happened that persistence in adhering to and in enforcing such monopolies has led, first, to attempts at regulation, and, these failing, to confiscation, and sometimes to the proscription of the owners. An example of such a phenomenon occurs to me which, just now, seems apposite.

In the earlier Middle Ages, before gunpowder made fortified houses untenable when attacked by the sovereign, the highways were so dangerous that trade and manufactures could only survive in walled towns. An unarmed urban population had to buy its privileges, and to pay for these a syndicate grew up in each town, which became responsible for the town ferm, or tax, and, in return, collected what part of the municipal expenses it could from the poorer inhabitants. These syndicates, called guilds, as a means of raising money, regulated trade and fixed prices, and they succeeded in fixing prices because they could prevent competition within the walls. Presently complaints became rife of guild oppression, and the courts had to entertain these complaints from the outset, to keep some semblance of order; but at length the turmoil passed beyond the reach of the courts, and Parliament intervened. Parliament not only enacted a series of statutes regulating prices in towns, but supervised guild membership, requiring trading companies to receive new members upon what Parliament considered to be reasonable terms. Nevertheless, friction continued.

With advances in science, artillery improved, and, as artillery improved, the police strengthened until the king could arrest whom he pleased. Then the country grew safe and manufactures migrated from the walled and heavily taxed towns to the cheap, open villages, and from thence undersold the guilds. As the area of competition broadened, so the guilds weakened, until, under Edward VI, being no longer able to defend themselves, they were ruthlessly and savagely plundered; and fifty years later the Court of King's Bench gravely held that a royal grant of a monopoly had always been bad at common law.[1]

Though the Court's law proved to be good, since it has stood, its history was fantastic; for the trade-guild was the offspring of trade monopoly, and a trade monopoly had for centuries been granted habitually by the feudal landlord to his tenants, and indeed was the only means by which an urban population could finance its military expenditure. Then, in due course, the Crown tried to establish its exclusive right to

[1] Darcy v. Allein, 11 Rep. 84.

grant monopolies, and finally Parliament — or King, Lords, and Commons combined, being the whole nation in its corporate capacity, — appropriated this monopoly of monopolies as its supreme prerogative. And with Parliament this monopoly has ever since remained.

In fine, monopolies, or competition in trade, appear to be recurrent social phases which depend upon the ratio which the mass and the fluidity of capital, or, in other words, its energy, bears to the area within which competition is possible. In the Middle Ages, when the town walls bounded that area, or when, at most, it was restricted to a few lines of communication between defensible points garrisoned by the monopolists, — as were the Staple towns of England which carried on the wool trade with the British fortified counting-houses in Flanders, — a small quantity of sluggish capital sufficed. But as police improved, and the area of competition broadened faster than capital accumulated and quickened, the competitive phase dawned, whose advent is marked by Darcy *v.* Allein, decided in the year 1600. Finally, the issue between monopoly and free trade was fought out in the American Revolution, for the measure which precipitated hostilities was the effort of England to impose her monopoly of the Eastern trade upon America. The Boston Tea Party occurred on December 16, 1773. Then came the heyday of competition with the acceptance of the theories of Adam Smith, and the political domination in England, towards 1840, of the Manchester school of political economy.

About forty years since, in America at least, the tide would appear once more to have turned. I fix the moment of flux, as I am apt to do, by a lawsuit. This suit was the Morris Run Coal Company *v.* Barclay Coal Company,[1] which is the first modern anti-monopoly litigation that I have met with in the United States. It was decided in Pennsylvania in 1871; and since 1871, while the area within which competition is possible has been kept constant by the tariff, capital has accumulated and has been concentrated and volatilized until, within this republic, substantially all prices are fixed by a vast moneyed mass. This mass, obeying what amounts to being a single volition, has its heart in Wall Street, and pervades every corner of the Union. No matter

[1] 68 Pa. 173.

what price is in question, whether it be the price of meat, or coal, or cotton cloth, or of railway transportation, or of insurance, or of discounts, the inquirer will find the price to be, in essence, a monopoly or fixed price; and if he will follow his investigation to the end, he will also find that the first cause in the complex chain of cause and effect which created the monopoly is that mysterious energy which is enthroned on the Hudson.

The presence of monopolistic prices in trade is not always a result of conscious agreement; more frequently, perhaps, it is automatic, and is an effect of the concentration of capital to a point where competition ceases, as when all the capital engaged in a trade belongs to a single owner. Supposing ownership to be enough restricted, combination is easier and more profitable than competition; therefore combination, conscious or unconscious, supplants competition. The inference from the evidence is that, in the United States, capital has reached, or is rapidly reaching, this point of concentration; and if this be true, competition cannot be enforced by legislation. But, assuming that competition could still be enforced by law, the only effect would be to make the mass of capital more homogeneous by eliminating still further such of the weaker capitalists as have survived. Ultimately, unless indeed society is to dissolve and capital migrate elsewhere, all the present phenomena would be intensified. Nor would free trade, probably, have more than a very transitory effect. In no department of trade is competition freer than in the Atlantic passenger service, and yet in no trade is there a stricter monopoly price.

The same acceleration of the social movement which has caused this centralization of capital has caused the centralization of another form of human energy, which is its negative: labor unions organize labor as a monopoly. Labor protests against the irresponsible sovereignty of capital, as men have always protested against irresponsible sovereignty, declaring that the capitalistic social system, as it now exists, is a form of slavery. Very logically, therefore, the abler and bolder labor agitators proclaim that labor levies actual war against society, and that in that war there can be no truce until irresponsible capital has capitulated. Also, in labor's methods of warfare the same phenomena appear as in the autocracy of capital. Labor attacks capitalistic society by methods beyond the purview of the law, and may, at any moment, shatter the social system; while, under our laws and institutions, society is helpless.

Few persons, I should imagine, who reflect on these phenomena, fail to admit to themselves, whatever they may say publicly, that present social conditions are unsatisfactory, and I take the cause of the stress to be that which I have stated. We have extended the range of applied science until we daily use infinite forces, and those forces must, apparently, disrupt our society, unless we can raise the laws and institutions which hold society together to an energy and efficiency commensurate to them. How much vigor and ability would be required to accomplish such a work may be measured by the experience of Washington, who barely prevailed in his relatively simple task, surrounded by a generation of extraordinary men, and with the capitalistic class of America behind him. Without the capitalistic class he must have failed. Therefore one most momentous problem of the future is the attitude which capital can or will assume in this emergency.

That some of the more sagacious of the capitalistic class have preserved that instinct of self-preservation which was so conspicuous among men of the type of Washington, is apparent from the position taken by the management of the United States Steel Company, and by the Republican minority of the Congressional Committee which recently investigated the Steel Company; but whether such men very strongly influence the genus to which they belong is not clear. If they do not, much improvement in existing conditions can hardly be anticipated.

If capital insists upon continuing to exercise sovereign powers, without accepting responsibility as for a trust, the revolt against the existing order must probably continue, and that revolt can only be dealt with, as all servile revolts must be dealt with, by physical force. I doubt, however, if even the most ardent and optimistic of capitalists would care to speculate deeply upon the stability of any government capital might organize, which rested on the fundamental principle that the American people must be ruled by an army. On the other hand any government to be effective must be strong. It is futile to talk of keeping peace in labor disputes by compulsory arbitration, if the government has not the power to command obedience to its arbitrators' decree; but a government able to constrain a couple of hundred thousand discontented railway employees to work against their will, must differ considerably from the one we have. Nor is it possible to imagine that labor will ever yield peaceful obedience to such constraint, unless capital makes equivalent concessions, — unless, perhaps, among other things, capital consents to erect tribunals which shall offer relief to any citizen who can show himself to be oppressed by the monopolistic price. In fine, a government, to promise stability in the future, must apparently be so much more powerful than any private interest, that all men will stand equally before its tribunals; and these tribunals must be flexible enough to reach those categories of activity which now lie beyond legal jurisdiction.

If it be objected that the American people are incapable of an effort so prodigious, I readily admit that this may be true, but I also contend that the objection is beside the issue. What the American people can or cannot do is a matter of opinion, but that social changes are imminent appears to be almost certain. Though these changes cannot be prevented, possibly they may, to a degree, be guided, as Washington guided the changes of 1789. To resist them perversely, as they were resisted at the Chicago Convention of 1912, can only make the catastrophe, when it comes, as overwhelming as was the consequent defeat of the Republican party.

Approached thus, that Convention of 1912 has more than a passing importance, since it would seem to indicate the ordinary phenomenon, that a declining favored class is incapable of appreciating an approaching change of environment which must alter its social status. I began with the proposition that, in any society which we now understand, civilization is equivalent to order, and the evidence of the truth of the proposition is, that amidst disorder, capital and credit, which constitute the pith of our civilization, perish first. For more than a century past, capital and credit have been absolute, or nearly so; accordingly it has not been the martial type which has enjoyed sovereignty, but the capitalistic. The warrior has been the capitalists' servant. But now, if it be true that money, in certain crucial directions, is losing its purchasing power, it is evident that capitalists must accept a position of equality before the law under the domination of a type of man who can enforce obedience; their own obedience, as well as the obedience of others. Indeed, it might occur, even to some optimists, that capitalists would be fortunate if they could certainly obtain protection for another fifty years on terms as favorable as these. But at Chicago, capitalists declined even to consider receding to a secondary position. Rather than permit the advent of a power beyond their immediate control, they preferred to shatter the instrument by which they sustained their ascendancy. For it is clear that Roosevelt's offence in the eyes of the capitalistic class was not what he had actually done, for he had done nothing seriously to injure them. The crime they resented was the assertion of the principle of equality before the law, for equality before the law signified the end of privilege to operate beyond the range of law. If this principle which Roosevelt, in theory at least, certainly embodied, came to be rigorously enforced, capitalists perceived that private persons would be precluded from using the functions of sovereignty to enrich themselves. There lay the parting of the ways. Sooner or later almost every successive ruling class has had this dilemma in one of its innumerable forms presented to them, and few have had the genius to compromise while compromise was possible. Only a generation ago the aristocracy of the South deliberately chose a civil war rather than admit the principle that at some future day they might have to accept compensation for their slaves.

A thousand other instances of similar incapacity might be adduced, but I will content myself with this alone.

Briefly the precedents induce the inference that privileged classes seldom have the intelligence to protect themselves by adaptation when nature turns against them, and, up to the present moment, the old privileged class in the United States has shown little promise of being an exception to the rule.

Be this, however, as it may, and even assuming that the great industrial and capitalistic interests would be prepared to assist a movement toward consolidation, as their ancestors assisted Washington, I deem it far from probable that they could succeed with the large

American middle class, which naturally should aid, opposed, as it seems now to be, to such a movement. Partially, doubtless, this opposition is born of fear, since the lesser folk have learned by bitter experience that the powerful have yielded to nothing save force, and therefore that their only hope is to crush those who oppress them. Doubtless, also, there is the inertia incident to long tradition, but I suspect that the resistance is rather due to a subtle and, as yet, nearly unconscious instinct, which teaches the numerical majority, who are inimical to capital, that the shortest and easiest way for them to acquire autocratic authority is to obtain an absolute mastery over those political tribunals which we call courts. Also that mastery is being by them rapidly acquired. So long as our courts retain their present functions no comprehensive administrative reform is possible, whence I conclude that the relation which our courts shall hold to politics is now the fundamental problem which the American people must solve, before any stable social equilibrium can be attained.

Theodore Roosevelt's enemies have been many and bitter. They have attacked his honesty, his sobriety, his intelligence, and his judgment, but very few of them have hitherto denied that he has a keen instinct for political strife. Only of late has this gift been doubted, but now eminent politicians question whether he did not make a capital mistake when he presented the reform of our courts of law, as expounders of the Constitution, as one of his two chief issues, in his canvass for a nomination for a third presidential term.

After many years of study of, and reflection upon, this intricate subject I have reached the conviction that, though Mr. Roosevelt may have erred in the remedy which he has suggested, he is right in the principle which he has advanced, and in my next chapter I propose to give the evidence and explain the reasons which constrain me to believe that American society must continue to degenerate until confusion supervenes, if our courts shall remain semipolitical chambers.

CHAPTER II

THE LIMITATIONS OF THE JUDICIAL FUNCTION

Taking the human race collectively, its ideal of a court of justice has been the omniscient and inexorable judgment seat of God. Individually, on the contrary, they have dearly loved favor. Hence the doctrine of the Intercession of the Saints, which many devout persons have sincerely believed could be bought by them for money. The whole development of civilization may be followed in the oscillation of any given society between these two extremes, the many always striving to so restrain the judiciary that it shall be unable to work the will of the favored few. On the whole, success in attaining to ideal justice has not been quite commensurate with the time and effort devoted to solving the problem, but, until our constitutional experiment was tried in America, I think it had been pretty generally admitted that the first prerequisite to success was that judges should be removed from political influences. For the main difficulty has been that every dominant class, as it has arisen, has done its best to use the machinery of justice for its own benefit.

No argument ever has convinced like a parable, and a very famous story in the Bible will illustrate the great truth, which is the first lesson that a primitive people learns, that unless the judge can be separated from the sovereign, and be strictly limited in the performance of his functions by a recognized code of procedure, the public, as against the dominant class, has, in substance, no civil rights. The kings of Israel were judges of last resort. Solomon earned his reputation for wisdom in the cause in which two mothers claimed the same child. They were indeed both judge and jury. Also they were prosecuting officers. Also they were sheriffs. In fine they exercised unlimited judicial power, save in so far as they were checked by the divine interference usually signified through some prophet.

Now David was, admittedly, one of the best sovereigns and judges who ever held office in Jerusalem, and, in the days of David, Nathan was the leading prophet of the dominant political party.

"And it came to pass in an eveningtide, that David arose from off his bed, and walked upon the roof of the king's house: and from the roof he saw a woman washing herself; and the woman was very beautiful to look upon. And David sent and enquired after the woman. And one said, Is not this Bath-sheba, the daughter of Eliam, the wife of Uriah the Hittite? And David sent messengers, and took her; and she came in unto him, and he lay with her; . . . and she returned unto her house."

Uriah was serving in the army under Joab. David sent for Uriah, and told him to go home to his wife, but Uriah refused. Then David wrote a letter to Joab and dismissed Uriah, ordering him to give the letter to Joab. And David "wrote in the letter, saying, Set ye Uriah in the forefront of the hottest battle, and retire ye from him, that he may be smitten and die. . . .

"And the men of the city went out and fought with Joab; and there fell some of the people of the servants of David; and Uriah the Hittite died also. . . . But the thing that David had done displeased the Lord.

"And the Lord sent Nathan unto David. And

he came unto him, and said unto him, There were two men in one city; the one rich and the other poor. The rich man had exceeding many flocks and herds:

"But the poor man had nothing, save one little ewe lamb, which he had bought and nourished up: and it grew up together with him, and with his children; it did eat of his own meat and drank of his own cup, and lay in his bosom, and was unto him as a daughter.

"And there came a traveller unto the rich man, and he spared to take of his own flock, . . . but took the poor man's lamb, and dressed it for the man that was come to him.

"And David's anger was greatly kindled against the man; and he said to Nathan, As the Lord liveth, the man that hath done this thing shall surely die: . . .

"And Nathan said to David, Thou art the man. Thus saith the Lord God of Israel. . . . Now therefore the sword shall never depart from thine house; because thou has despised me. . . . Behold, I will raise up evil against thee out of thine own house, and I will take thy wives before thine eyes, and give them unto thy neighbor."

Here, as the heading to the Twelfth Chapter of Second Book of Samuel says, "Nathan's parable of the ewe lamb causeth David to be his own judge," but the significant part of the story is that Nathan, with all his influence, could not force David to surrender his prey. David begged very hard to have his sentence remitted, but, for all that, "David sent and fetched [Bathsheba] to his house, and she became his wife, and bare him a son." Indeed, she bore him Solomon. As against David or David's important supporters men like Uriah had no civil rights that could be enforced.

Even after the judicial function is nominally severed from the executive function, so that the sovereign himself does not, like David and Solomon, personally administer justice, the same result is reached through agents, as long as the judge holds his office at the will of the chief of a political party.

To go no farther afield, every page of English history blazons this record. Long after the law had taken an almost modern shape, Alice Perrers, the mistress of Edward III, sat on the bench at Westminster and intimidated the judges into deciding for suitors who had secured her services.

The chief revenue of the rival factions during the War of the Roses was derived from attainders, indictments for treason, and forfeitures, avowedly partisan. Henry VII used the Star Chamber to ruin the remnants of the feudal aristocracy. Henry VIII exterminated as vagrants the wretched monks whom he had evicted. The prosecutions under Charles I largely induced the Great Rebellion; and finally the limit of endurance was reached when Charles II made Jeffreys Chief Justice of England in order to kill those who were prominent in opposition. Charles knew what he was doing. "That man," said he of Jeffreys, "has no learning, no sense, no manners, and more impudence than ten carted street-walkers." The first object was to convict Algernon Sidney of treason. Jeffreys used simple means. Usually drunk, his court resembled the den of a wild beast. He poured forth on "plaintiffs and defendants, barristers and attorneys, witnesses and jurymen, torrents of frantic abuse, intermixed with oaths and curses." The law required proof of an *overt act* of treason. Many years before Sidney had written a philosophical treatise touching resistance by the subject to the sovereign, as a constitutional principle. But, though the fragment contained nothing more than the doctrines of Locke, Sidney had cautiously shown it to no one, and it had only been found by searching his study. Jeffreys told the jury that if they believed the book to be Sidney's book, written by him, they must convict for *scribere est agere*, to write is to commit an overt act.

A revolution followed upon this and other like convictions, as revolutions have usually followed such uses of the judicial power. In that revolution the principle of the limitation of the judicial function was recognized, and the English people seriously addressed themselves to the task of separating their courts from political influences, of protecting their judges by making their tenure and their pay permanent, and of punishing them by removal if they behaved corruptly, or with prejudice, or transcended the limits within which their duty confined them. Jeffreys had legislated when he ruled it to be the law that, to write words secretly in one's closet, is to commit an overt act of treason, and he did it to kill a man whom the king who employed him wished to destroy. This was to transcend the duty of a judge, which is to expound and not to legislate. The judge may develop a principle, he may admit evidence of a custom in order to explain the intentions of the parties to a suit, as Lord Mansfield admitted evidence of the customs of merchants, but he should not legislate. To do so, as Jeffreys did in Sidney's case, is tantamount to murder. Jeffreys never was duly punished for his crimes. He died the year after the Revolution, in the Tower, maintaining to the last that he was innocent in the sight of God and man because "all the blood he had shed fell short of the King's command."

And Jeffreys was perfectly logical and consistent in his attitude. A judiciary is either an end in itself or a means to an end. If it be designed to protect the civil rights of citizens indifferently, it must be free from pressure which will deflect it from this path, and it can only be protected from the severest possible pressure by being removed from politics, because politics is the struggle for ascendancy of a class or a majority. If, on the other hand, the judiciary is to serve as an instrument for advancing the fortunes of a majority or a dominant class, as David used the Jewish judiciary, or as the Stuarts used the English judiciary, then the judicial power must be embodied either in a military or political leader, like David, who does the work himself, or in an agent, more or less like Jeffreys, who will obey his orders. In the colonies the subserviency of the judges to the Crown had been a standing grievance, and the result of this long and terrible experience, stretching through centuries both in Europe and America, had been to inspire Americans with a fear of intrusting power to any man or body of men. They sought to limit everything by written restrictions. Setting aside the objection that such a system is mechanically vicious because it involves excessive friction and therefore waste of energy, it is obviously futile unless the written restrictions can be enforced, and enforced in the spirit in which they are drawn. Hamilton, whose instinct for law resembled genius, saw the difficulty and pointed out in the *Federalist* that it is not a writing which can give protection, but only the intelligence and the sense of justice of the community itself.

"The truth is, that the general genius of a Government is all that can be substantially relied upon for permanent effects. Particular provisions, though not altogether useless, have far less virtue and efficiency than are commonly ascribed to them; and the want of them will never be, with men of sound discernment, a decisive objection to any plan which exhibits the leading characters of a good Government." After an experience of nearly a century and a quarter we must admit, I think, that Hamilton was right. In the United States we have carried bills of right and constitutional limitations to an extreme, and yet, I suppose that few would care to maintain that, during the nineteenth century, life and property were safer in America, or crime better dealt with, than in England, France, or Germany. The contrary, indeed, I take to be the truth, and I think one chief cause of this imperfection in the administration of justice will be found to have been the operation of the written Constitution. For, under the American system, the Constitution, or fundamental law, is expounded by judges, and this function, which, in essence, is political, has brought precisely that quality of pressure on the bench which it has been the labor of a hundred generations of our ancestors to remove. On the whole the result has been not to elevate politics, but to lower the courts toward the political level, a result which conforms to the *a priori* theory.

The abstract virtue of the written Constitution was not, however, a question in issue when Washington and his contemporaries set themselves to reorganize the Confederation. Those men had no choice but to draft some kind of a platform on which the states could agree to unite, if they were to unite peacefully at all, and accordingly they met in convention and drew the best form of agreement they could; but I more than suspect that a good many very able Federalists were quite alive to the defects in the plan which they adopted.

Hamilton was outspoken in preferring the English model, and I am not aware that Washington ever expressed a preference for the theory that, because of a written fundamental law, the court should nullify legislation. Nor is it unworthy of remark that all foreigners, after a prolonged and attentive observation of our experiment, have avoided it. Since 1789, every highly civilized Western people have readjusted their institutions at least once, yet not one has in this respect imitated us, though all have borrowed freely from the parliamentary system of England.[1]

Even our neighbor, Canada, with no adverse traditions and a population similar to ours, has been no exception to the rule. The Canadian courts indeed define the limits of provincial and federal jurisdiction as fixed under an act of Parliament, but they do not pretend to limit the exercise of power when the seat of power has been established. I take the cause of this distrust to be obvious. Although our written Constitution was successful in its primary purpose of facilitating the consolidation of the Confederation, it has not otherwise inspired confidence as a practical administrative device. Not only has constant judicial interference dislocated scientific legislation, but casting the judiciary into the vortex of civil faction has degraded it in the popular esteem. In fine, from the outset, the American bench, because it deals with the most fiercely contested of political issues, has been an instrument necessary to political success. Consequently, political

---

[1] The relation of courts to legislation in European countries has been pretty fully considered by Brinton Coxe, in *Judicial Power and Constitutional Legislation*.

parties have striven to control it, and therefore the bench has always had an avowed partisan bias. This avowed political or social bias has, I infer, bred among the American people the conviction that justice is not administered indifferently to all men, wherefore the bench is not respected with us as, for instance, it is in Great Britain, where law and politics are sundered. Nor has the dissatisfaction engendered by these causes been concealed. On the contrary, it has found expression through a series of famous popular leaders from Thomas Jefferson to Theodore Roosevelt.

The Constitution could hardly have been adopted or the government organized but for the personal influence of Washington, whose power lay in his genius for dealing with men. He lost no time or strength in speculation, but, taking the Constitution as the best implement at hand, he went to the work of administration by including the representatives of the antagonistic extremes in his Cabinet. He might as well have expected fire and water to mingle as Jefferson and Hamilton to harmonize. Probably he had no delusions on that head when he chose them

LIMITATIONS OF THE JUDICIAL FUNCTION 49

for his ministers, and he accomplished his object. He paralyzed opposition until the new mechanism began to operate pretty regularly, but he had not an hour to spare. Soon the French Revolution heated passions so hot that long before Washington's successor was elected the United States was rent by faction.

The question which underlay all other questions, down to the Civil War, was the determination of the seat of sovereignty. Hamilton and the Federalists held it to be axiomatic that, if the federal government were to be more than a shadow, it must interpret the meaning of the instrument which created it, and, if so, that it must signify its decisions through the courts. Only in this way, they argued, could written limitations on legislative power be made effective. Only in this way could statutes which contravened the Constitution be set aside.[1]

Jefferson was abroad when Hamilton wrote *The Federalist*, but his views have since been so universally accepted as embodying the opposition to Hamilton, that they may be conveniently taken as if they had been published while the Constitu-

[1] *Federalist*, No. LXXVIII.

tion was under discussion. Substantially the same arguments were advanced by others during the actual debate, if not quite so lucidly or connectedly then, as afterward by him.

Very well, said Jefferson, in answer to Hamilton, admitting, for the moment, that the central government shall define its own powers, and that the courts shall be the organ through which the exposition shall be made, both of which propositions I vehemently deny, you have this result: The judges who will be called upon to pass upon the validity of national and state legislation will be plunged in the most heated of controversies, and in those controversies they cannot fail to be influenced by the same passions and prejudices which sway other men. In a word they must decide like legislators, though they will be exempt from the responsibility to the public which controls other legislators. Such conditions you can only meet by making the judicial tenure of office ephemeral, as all legislative tenure is ephemeral.

It is vain to pretend, continued he, in support of fixity of tenure, that the greater the pressure on the judge is likely to be, the more need there is to make him secure. This may be true of judges clothed with ordinary attributes, like English judges, for, should these try to nullify the popular will by construing away statutes, Parliament can instantly correct them, or if Parliament fail in its duty, the constituencies, at the next election, can intervene. But no one will be able to correct the American judge who may decline to recognize the law which would constrain him. Nothing can shake him save impeachment for what is tantamount to crime, or being overruled by a constitutional amendment which you have purposely made too hard to obtain to be a remedy. He is to be judge in his own case without an appeal.

Nowhere in all his long and masterly defence of the Constitution did Hamilton show so much embarrassment as here, and because, probably, he did not himself believe in his own brief. He really had faith in the English principle of an absolute parliament, restrained, if needful, by a conservative chamber, like the House of Lords, but not in the total suspension of sovereignty subject to judicial illumination. Consequently he fell back on platitudes about judicial high-mindedness, and how judges could be trusted not to allow political influences to weigh with them when deciding political questions. Pushed to its logical end, concluded he, the Jeffersonian argument would prove that there should be no judges distinct from legislatures.[1]

Now, at length, exclaimed the Jeffersonian in triumph, you admit our thesis. You propose to clothe judges with the highest legislative functions, since you give them an absolute negative on legislation, and yet you decline to impose on them the responsibility to a constituency, which constrains other legislators. Clearly you thus make them autocratic, and in the worst sense, for you permit small bodies of irresponsibile men under pretence of dispensing justice, but really in a spirit of hypocrisy, to annul the will of the majority of the people, even though the right of the people to exercise their will, in the matters at issue, be clearly granted them in the Constitution.

No, rejoined Hamilton, thus driven to the wall, judges never will so abuse their trust. The duty of the judge requires him to suppress his *will*, and exercise his *judgment* only. The Constitution will be before him, and he will have only to say

[1] *The Federalist*, No. LXXVIII.

LIMITATIONS OF THE JUDICIAL FUNCTION

whether authority to legislate on a given subject is granted in that instrument. If it be, the character of the legislation must remain a matter of legislative discretion. Besides, you must repose confidence somewhere, and judges, on the whole, are more trustworthy than legislators. How can you say that, retorted the opposition, when you, better than most men, know the line of despotic legal precedents from the Ship Money down to the Writs of Assistance?

Looking back upon this initial controversy touching judicial functions under the Constitution, we can hardly suppose that Hamilton did not perceive that, in substance, Jefferson was right, and that a bench purposely constructed to pass upon political questions must be politically partisan. He knew very well that, if the Federalists prevailed in the elections, a Federalist President would only appoint magistrates who could be relied on to favor consolidation. And so the event proved. General Washington chose John Jay for the first Chief Justice, who in some important respects was more Federalist than Hamilton, while John Adams selected John Marshall, who, though one of the greatest jurists who ever lived, was hated by Jefferson with a bitter hatred, because of his political bias. As time went on matters grew worse. Before Marshall died slavery had become a burning issue, and the slave-owners controlled the appointing power. General Jackson appointed Taney to sustain the expansion of slavery, and when the anti-slavery party carried the country with Lincoln, Lincoln supplanted Taney with Chase, in order that Chase might stand by him in his struggle to destroy slavery. And as it has been, so must it always be. As long as the power to enact laws shall hinge on the complexion of benches of judges, so long will the ability to control a majority of the bench be as crucial a political necessity as the ability to control a majority in avowedly representative assemblies.

Hamilton was one of the few great jurists and administrators whom America has ever produced, and it is inconceivable that he did not understand what he was doing. He knew perfectly well that, other things being equal, the simplest administrative mechanism is the best, and he knew also that he was helping to make an extremely complicated mechanism. Not only so, but at the heart of this complexity lay the gigantic cog of the

LIMITATIONS OF THE JUDICIAL FUNCTION 55

judiciary, which was obviously devised to stop movement. He must have had a reason, beyond the reason he gave, for not only insisting on clothing the judiciary with these unusual political and legislative attributes, but for giving the judiciary an unprecedented fixity of tenure. I suspect that he was actuated by some such considerations as these:

The Federalists, having pretty good cause to suppose themselves in a popular minority, purposed to consolidate the thirteen states under a new sovereign. There were but two methods by which they could prevail; they could use force, or, to secure assent, they could propose some system of arbitration. To escape war the Federalists convened the constitutional convention, and by so doing pledged themselves to arbitration. But if their plan of consolidation were to succeed, it was plain that the arbitrator must arbitrate in their favor, for if he arbitrated as Mr. Jefferson would have wished, the United States under the Constitution would have differed little from the United States under the Confederation. The Federalists, therefore, must control the arbitrator. If the Constitution were to be adopted, Hamilton and every one else knew that Washington would be the first President, and Washington could be relied on to appoint a strong Federalist bench. Hence, whatever might happen subsequently, when the new plan first should go into operation, and when the danger from insubordination among the states would probably be most acute, the judiciary would be made to throw its weight in favor of consolidation, and against disintegration, and, if it did so, it was essential that it should be protected against anything short of a revolutionary attack.

In the convention, indeed, Charles Pinckney of South Carolina suggested that Congress should be empowered to negative state legislation, but such an alternative, for obvious reasons, would have been less palatable to Hamilton, since Congress would be only too likely to fall under the control of the Jeffersonian party, while a bench of judges, if once well chosen, might prove to be for many years an "excellent barrier to the encroachments and oppressions of the representative body."[1]

I infer that Hamilton and many other Federalists reasoned somewhat thus, not only from what

[1] *The Federalist*, No. LXXVIII.

LIMITATIONS OF THE JUDICIAL FUNCTION

they wrote, but from the temper of their minds, and, if they did, events largely justified them. John Jay, Oliver Ellsworth, and John Marshall were successively appointed to the office of Chief Justice, nor did the complexion of the Supreme Court change until after 1830.

What interests us, however, is not so much what the Federalists thought, or the motives which actuated them, as the effect which the clothing of the judiciary with political functions has had upon the development of the American republic, more especially as that extreme measure might have been avoided, had Pinckney's plan been adopted. Nor, looking back upon the actual course of events, can I perceive that, so far as the movement toward consolidation was concerned, the final result would have varied materially whether Congress or the Supreme Court had exercised control over state legislation. Marshall might just as well, in the one case as the other, have formulated his theory of a semi-centralized administration. He would only have had uniformly to sustain Congress, as an English judge sustains Parliament. Nor could either Congress or the Court have reached a definite result without an appeal to force. Either chamber might expound a theory, but nothing save an army could establish it.

For two generations statesmen and jurists debated the relation of the central to the local sovereignties with no result, for words alone could decide no such issue. In America, as elsewhere, sovereignty is determined by physical force. Marshall could not conquer Jefferson, he could at most controvert Jefferson's theory. This he did, but, in doing so, I doubt if he were quite true to himself. Jefferson contended that every state might nullify national legislation, as conversely Pinckney wished Congress to be given explicitly the power to nullify state legislation; and Marshall, very sensibly, pointed out that, were Jefferson's claim carried into practice, it would create "a hydra in government,"[1] yet I am confident that Marshall did not appreciate whither his own assertion of authority must lead. In view of the victory of centralization in the Civil War, I will agree that the Supreme Court might have successfully maintained a position as arbitrator touching conflicting juris-

[1] Cohens v. Virginia, 6 Wheaton 415.

LIMITATIONS OF THE JUDICIAL FUNCTION

dictions, as between the nation and the states, but that is a different matter from assuming to examine into the wisdom of the legislation itself. The one function might, possibly, pass by courtesy as judicial; the other is clearly legislative.

This distinction only developed after Marshall's death, but the resentment which impelled Marshall to annul an act of Congress was roused by the political conflict which preceded the election of 1800, in which Marshall took a chief part. Apparently he could not resist the temptation of measuring himself with his old adversary, especially as he seems to have thought that he could discredit that adversary without giving him an opportunity to retaliate.

In 1798 a Federalist Congress passed the Alien and Sedition Acts, whose constitutionality no Federalist judge ever doubted, but which Jefferson considered as clearly a violation of the fundamental compact, since they tended to drive certain states, as he thought, into "revolution and blood." Under this provocation Jefferson proclaimed that it was both the right and the duty of any state, which felt itself aggrieved, to intervene to arrest "the progress of the evil," within her territory, by declining to execute, or by "nullifying," the objectionable statutes. As Jefferson wrote the Kentucky Resolutions in 1798 and was elected President in 1800, the people at least appeared to have sustained him in his exposition of the Constitution, before he entered into office.

At this distance of time we find it hard to realize what the election of 1800 seemed to portend to those who participated therein. Mr. Jefferson always described it as amounting to a revolution as profound as, if less bloody than, the revolution of 1776, and though we may be disposed to imagine that Jefferson valued his own advent to power at its full worth, it must be admitted that his enemies regarded it almost as seriously. Nor were they without some justification, for Jefferson certainly represented the party of disintegration. "Nullification" would have been tantamount to a return to the condition of the Confederation. Besides, Jefferson not so many years before had written, in defence of Shays's rebellion, that the tree of Liberty could never flourish unless refreshed occasionally with the blood of patriots and tyrants. To most Federalists Jefferson seemed a bloodthirsty demagogue.

In 1796 Oliver Ellsworth had been appointed Chief Justice by General Washington in the place of Jay, who resigned, and in 1799 John Adams sent Ellsworth as an envoy to France to try to negotiate a treaty which should reëstablish peace between the two countries. Ellsworth succeeded in his mission, but the hardships of his journey injured his health, and he, in turn, resigned in the autumn of 1800. Then Adams offered the Chief Justiceship to Jay, but Jay would not return to office, and after this the President selected his Secretary of State, John Marshall, one of the greatest of the great Virginians, but one of Jefferson's most irreconcilable enemies. Perhaps at no moment in his life did John Adams demonstrate his legal genius more convincingly than in this remarkable nomination. Yet it must be conceded that, in making John Marshall Chief Justice, John Adams deliberately chose the man whom, of all his countrymen, he thought to be the most formidable champion of those views which he himself entertained, and which he conceived that he had been elected President to advance. Nor was John Adams deceived. For thirty-four years John Marshall labored ceaselessly to counteract Jefferson's constitutional principles, while Jefferson always denounced the political partiality of the federal courts, and above all the "rancorous hatred which Marshall bears to the government of his country, and . . . the cunning and sophistry within which he is able to enshroud himself."[1]

No one, at this day, would be disposed to dispute that the Constitution, as a device to postpone war among the states, at least for a period, was successful, and that, as I have already pointed out, during the tentative interval which extended until Appomattox, the Supreme Court served perhaps as well, in ordinary times, as an arbiter between the states and the general government, as any which could have been suggested. So much may be conceded, and yet it remains true, as the record will show, that when it passed this point and entered into factional strife, the Supreme Court somewhat lamentably failed, probably injuring itself and popular respect for law, far more by its errors, than it aided the Union by its political adjudications.

Although John Marshall, by common consent,

[1] To Madison, Ford, 9, 275.

ranks as one of the greatest and purest of Americans, yet even Marshall had human weaknesses, one of which was a really unreasonable antipathy to Thomas Jefferson; an antipathy which, I surmise, must, when Jefferson was inaugurated, have verged upon contempt. At least Marshall did what cautious men seldom do when they respect an adversary, he took the first opportunity to pick a quarrel with a man who had the advantage of him in position.

In the last days of his presidency John Adams appointed one William Marbury a justice of the peace for the District of Columbia. The Senate confirmed the appointment, and the President signed, and John Marshall, as Secretary of State, sealed Marbury's commission; but in the hurry of surrendering office the commission was not delivered, and Jefferson found it in the State Department when he took possession. Resenting violently these "midnight" appointments, as he called them, Jefferson directed Mr. Madison, his Secretary of State, to withhold the commission; and, at the next December term of the Supreme Court, Marbury moved for a rule to Madison to show cause why he should not be commanded to deliver to the plaintiff the property to which Marbury pretended to be entitled. Of course Jefferson declined to appear before Marshall, through his Secretary of State, and finally, in February, 1803, Marshall gave judgment, in what was, without any doubt, the most anomalous opinion he ever delivered, in that it violated all judicial conventions, for, apparently, no object, save to humiliate a political opponent.

Marshall had no intention of commanding Madison to surrender the commission to Marbury. He was too adroit a politician for that. Marshall knew that he could not compel Jefferson to obey such a writ against his will, and that in issuing the order he would only bring himself and his court into contempt. What he seems to have wished to do was to give Jefferson a lesson in deportment. Accordingly, instead of dismissing Marbury's suit upon any convenient pretext, as, according to legal etiquette, he should have done if he had made up his mind to decide against the plaintiff, and yet thought it inexpedient to explain his view of the law, he began his opinion with a long and extra-judicial homily, first on Marbury's title to ownership in the commission, and then on civil liberty. Having affirmed that Marbury's right to his office vested when the President had signed, and the Secretary of State had sealed the instrument, he pointed out that withholding the property thus vested was a violation of civil rights which could be examined in a court of justice. Were it otherwise, the Chief Justice insisted, the government of the United States could not be termed a government of laws and not of men.

All this elaborate introduction was in the nature of a solemn lecture by the Chief Justice of the Supreme Court to the President of the United States upon his faulty discharge of his official duties. Having eased his mind on this head, Marshall went on, very dexterously indeed, but also very palpably, to elude the consequences of his temerity. He continued: The right of property being established, and the violation of that right clear, it is plain that a wrong has been committed, and it only remains to determine whether that wrong can be redressed under this form of procedure. We are of opinion that it cannot, because Congress has no constitutional power to confer upon the Supreme Court original jurisdiction in this class of litigation. In the lower courts alone can the relief prayed for be obtained.

Of all the events of Marshall's life this controversy with Jefferson seems to me the most equivocal, and it was a direct effect of a constitutional system which has permitted the courts to become the censor of the political departments of the government. Marshall, probably, felt exasperated by Jefferson's virulence against these final appointments made by John Adams, while Marshall was Secretary of State, and for which he may have felt himself, in part, responsible. Possibly, even, he may have taken some of Jefferson's strictures as aimed at himself. At all events he went to extreme lengths in retaliation. He might have dismissed the litigation in a few words by stating that, whatever the abstract rights of the parties might have been, the Supreme Court had no power to constrain the President in his official functions; but he yielded to political animosity. Then, having taken a position practically untenable, he had to find an avenue of retreat, and he found it by asserting a supervisory jurisdiction over

Congress, a step which, even at that early period, was most hazardous.[1]

In reality Jefferson's temper, far from being vindictive and revolutionary, as his enemies believed, was rather gentle and timid, but he would have been more than mortal had he endured such an insult in silence. Nor could he, perhaps, have done so without risking the respect of his followers. So he decided on reprisals, and a scheme was matured among influential Virginians, like John Randolph and Senator William Giles, to purge the Supreme Court of Federalists. Among the associate justices of this court was Samuel Chase, a signer of the Declaration of Independence and an able lawyer, but an arrogant and indiscreet partisan. Chase had made himself obnoxious on various public occasions and so was considered to be the best subject to impeach; but if they succeeded with him the Jeffersonians proclaimed their intention of removing all his brethren seriatim, including the chief offender of all, John Marshall.

[1] Marshall's constitutional doctrine was not universally accepted, even in the courts of the northern states, until long afterward. As eminent a jurist as Chief Justice Gibson of Pennsylvania, as late as 1825, gave a very able dissenting opinion in opposition in Eakin *v.* Raub, 12 S. & R., 344.

One day in December, 1804, Senator Giles, of Virginia, in a conversation which John Quincy Adams has reported in his diary, discussed the issue at large, and that conversation is most apposite now, since it shows how early the inevitable tendency was developed to make judges who participate in political and social controversies responsible to the popular will. The conversation is too long to extract in full, but a few sentences will convey its purport: —

"He treated with the utmost contempt the idea of an *independent* judiciary. . . . And if the judges of the Supreme Court should dare, *as they had done*, to declare an act of Congress unconstitutional, or to send a mandamus to the Secretary of State, *as they had done*, it was the undoubted right of the House of Representatives to impeach them, and of the Senate to remove them, for giving such opinions, however honest or sincere they may have been in entertaining them. * * * And a removal by impeachment was nothing more than a declaration by Congress to this effect: You hold dangerous opinions, and if you are suffered to carry them into effect you will work the destruction of the nation. *We want your offices*, for the purpose of giving them to men who will fill them better." [1]

Jefferson, though he controlled a majority in the Senate, failed by a narrow margin to obtain the two-thirds vote necessary to convict Chase. Nevertheless, he accomplished his object. Chase never recovered his old assurance, and Marshall never again committed a solecism in judicial manners. On his side, after the impeachment, Jefferson showed moderation. He might, if he had been malevolent, without doubt, have obtained an act of Congress increasing the membership of the Supreme Court enough to have put Marshall in a minority. Then by appointing men like Giles he could have compelled Marshall to resign. He did nothing of the kind. He spared the Supreme Court, which he might have overthrown, and contented himself with waiting until time should give him the opportunity to correct the political tendencies of a body of men whom he sincerely regarded as a menace to, what he considered, popular institutions. Thus the ebullition caused by Marshall's acrimony toward Jefferson, because of Jefferson's strictures on the appoint-

[1] Memoirs, I, 322.

ments made by his predecessor subsided, leaving no very serious immediate mischief behind, save the precedent of the nullification of an act of Congress by the Supreme Court. That precedent, however, was followed by Marshall's Democratic successor. And nothing can better illustrate the inherent vice of the American constitutional system than that it should have been possible, in 1853, to devise and afterward present to a tribunal, whose primary purpose was to administer the municipal law, a set of facts for adjudication, on purpose to force it to pass upon the validity of such a statute as the Missouri Compromise, which had been enacted by Congress in 1820, as a sort of treaty of peace between the North and South, and whose object was the limitation of the spread of slavery. Whichever way the Court decided, it must have fallen into opprobrium with one-half the country. In fact, having been organized by the slaveholders to sustain slavery, it decided against the North, and therefore lost repute with the party destined to be victorious. I need not pause to criticise the animus of the Court, nor yet the quality of the law which the Chief Justice there laid down. It suffices that in the decade which preceded hostilities no event, in all probability, so exasperated passions, and so shook the faith of the people of the northern states in the judiciary, as this decision. Faith, whether in the priest or the magistrate, is of slow growth, and if once impaired is seldom fully restored. I doubt whether the Supreme Court has ever recovered from the shock it then received, and, considered from this point of view, the careless attitude of the American people toward General Grant's administration, when in 1871 it obtained the reversal of Hepburn v. Griswold by appointments to the bench, assumes a sombre aspect.

Of late some sensitiveness has been shown in regard to this transaction, and a disposition has appeared to defend General Grant and his Attorney-General against the charge of manipulating the membership of the bench to suit their own views. At the outset, therefore, I wish to disclaim any intention of entering into this discussion. To me it is immaterial whether General Grant and Mr. Hoar did or did not nominate judges with a view to obtaining a particular judgment. I am concerned not with what men thought, but with what they did, and with the effect of their acts at the moment, upon their fellow-citizens.

Hepburn v. Griswold was decided in conference on November 27, 1869, when eight justices were on the bench. On February 1, following, Justice Grier resigned, and, on February 7, judgment was entered, the court then being divided four to three, but Grier having been with the majority, the vote in reality stood five to three. Two vacancies therefore existed on February 7, one caused by the resignation of Grier, the other by an act of Congress which had enlarged the court by one member, and which had taken effect in the previous December.

Chief Justice Chase held that the clause of the currency laws of 1862 and 1863 which made depreciated paper a legal tender for preëxisting debts was unconstitutional. No sooner had the judgment been recorded than all the world perceived that, if both vacancies should be filled with men who would uphold the acts, Hepburn v. Griswold might be reversed by a majority of one.

The Republican party had full control of the government and was united in vehement support of the laws. On March 21, the second of the two new judges received his commission, and precisely ten days afterward the Attorney-General moved for a rehearing, taunting the Chief Justice with having changed his opinion on this point, and intimating that the issue was in reality political, and not judicial at all.

In the December Term following Knox v. Lee was argued by the Attorney-General, and, on May 1, 1871, judgment was entered reversing Hepburn v. Griswold, both the new judges voting with the former minority, thus creating the necessary majority of one. No one has ever doubted that what General Grant did coincided with the drift of opinion, and that the Republican party supported him without inquiring how he had achieved success.[1] After this it is difficult to suppose that much respect could remain among the American people for the sanctity of judicial political decisions, or that a President, at the head of a popular majority, would incur much odium for intervening to correct them, as a party measure.

The last example of judicial interference which

---

[1] Hepburn v. Griswold, 8 Wallace 603. Decided in conference on Nov. 27, 1869, more than a month before Grier's resignation. Knox v. Lee, 12 Wallace 457.

I shall mention was the nullification, in 1895, of a statute of Congress which imposed an income tax. The states have since set this decision aside by constitutional amendment, and I should suppose that few would now dispute that the Court when it so decided made a serious political and social error. As Mr. Justice White pointed out, the judges undertook to deprive the people, in their corporate capacity, of a power conceded to Congress "by universal consensus for one hundred years."[1] These words were used in the first argument, but on the rehearing the present Chief Justice waxed warm in remonstrating against the unfortunate position in which his brethren placed the Court before the nation, protesting with almost passionate earnestness against the reversal by half-a-dozen judges of what had been the universally accepted legal, political, and economic policy of the country solely in order that "invested wealth" might be read "into the constitution" as a favored and protected class of property. Mr. Justice White closed by saying that by this act the Supreme Court had "deprived [the Government] of an inherent attribute of its being."[2]

[1] 157 U. S. 608.
[2] Pollock v. The Farmers' Loan & Trust Co., 158 U. S. 715.

I might go on into endless detail, but I apprehend that these cases, which are the most important which have ever arisen on this issue, suffice for my purpose.[1] I contend that no court can, because of the nature of its being, effectively check a popular majority acting through a co-

[1] In 1889 Mr. J. C. Bancroft Davis compiled a table of the acts of Congress which up to that time had been held to be unconstitutional. It is to be found in the Appendix to volume 131 U. S. Reports, page ccxxxv. Mr. Davis has, however, omitted from his list the Dred Scott Case, probably for the technical reason that, in 1857, when the cause was decided, the Missouri Compromise had been repealed. Nevertheless, though this is true, Taney's decision hinged upon the invalidity of the law.

Besides the statutes which I have mentioned in the text, the two most important, I suppose, which have been annulled, have to me no little interest. These are the Civil Rights Act of 1875, and the Employers' Liability Act of 1906. The Civil Rights Act of 1875 grew rapidly unpopular, and the decision which overturned it coincided with the strong drift of opinion. The Civil Rights Cases were decided in October, 1883, and Mr. Cleveland was elected President in 1884. Doubtless the law would have been repealed had the judiciary supported it. Therefore this adjudication stood.

On the other hand, the Employers' Liability Act of 1906 was held bad because Congress undertook to deal with commerce conducted wholly within the states, and therefore beyond the national jurisdiction. The Court, consequently, in the Employers' Liability Cases, simply defined the limits of sovereignty, as a Canadian Court might do; it did not question the existence of sovereignty itself. In 1908 Congress passed a statute free from this objection, and the Court, in the Second Employers' Liability Cases, 223 U. S. 1, sustained the legislation in the most thoroughgoing manner. I know not where to look for two better illustrations of my theory.

ordinate legislative assembly, and I submit that the precedents which I have cited prove this contention. The only result of an attempt and failure is to bring courts of justice into odium or contempt, and, in any event, to make them objects of attack by a dominant social force in order to use them as an instrument, much as Charles II used Jeffreys.

The moment we consider the situation philosophically we perceive why using a court to control a coördinate legislature must, nearly inevitably, be sooner or later fatal to the court, if it asserts its prerogative. A court to be a fit tribunal to administer the municipal law impartially, or even relatively impartially, must be a small body of men, holding by a permanent and secure tenure, guarded from all pressure which may unduly influence them. Also they should be men of much experience and learned in the precedents which should make the rules which they apply stable and consistent. In short, a court should be rigid and emotionless. It follows that it must be conservative, for its members should long have passed that period of youth when the mind is sensitive to new impressions. Were it otherwise, law would cease to be cohesive.

A legislature is nearly the antithesis of a court. It is designed to reflect the passions of the voters, and the majority of voters are apt to be young. Hence in periods of change, when alone serious clashes between legislatures and courts are likely to occur, as the social equilibrium shifts the legislature almost certainly will reflect the rising, the court the sinking power. I take the Dred Scott Case as an illustration. In 1857 the slaveholding interest had passed the zenith of high fortune, and was hastening toward its decline. In the elections of 1858 the Democratic party, which represented slavery, was defeated. But the Supreme Court had been organized by Democrats who had been dominant for many years, and it adhered, on the principle laid down by Jeffreys, to the master which created it.

Occasionally, it is true, a court has been constructed by a rising energy, as was the Supreme Court in 1789, but then it is equally tenacious to the instinct which created it. The history of the Supreme Court is, in this point of view, eminently suggestive. The Federalist instinct was constructive, not destructive, and accordingly Marshall's fame rests on a series of constructive decisions like M'Culloch v. Maryland, Cohens v. Virginia, and Gibbons v. Odgen. In these decisions he either upheld actual national legislation, or else the power of the nation to legislate. Conversely, whenever Marshall or his successors have sought to obstruct social movement they have not prospered. Marbury v. Madison is not an episode on which any admirer of Marshall can linger with satisfaction. In theory it may be true, as Hamilton contended, that, given the fact that a written constitution is inevitable, a bench of judges is the best tribunal to interpret its meaning, since the duty of the judge has ever been and is now to interpret the meaning of written instruments; but it does not follow from this premise that the judges who should exercise this office should be the judges who administer the municipal law. In point of fact experience has proved that, so far as Congress is concerned, the results of judicial interference have been negative. And it would be well if in other spheres of American constitutional development, judicial activity had been always negative. Unfortunately, as I believe, it has extended into the domain of legislation. I will take the Dred Scott Case once more to illustrate my meaning. The North found it bad enough for the Supreme Court to hold that, under the Constitution, Congress could not exclude slavery from the national territory beyond a certain boundary which had been fixed by compromise between the North and South. But the North would have found it intolerable if the Court, while fully conceding that Congress might so legislate, if the character of the legislation commended itself to the judges, had held the Missouri Compromise to be unconstitutional because they thought it *unreasonable*. Yet this, in substance, is what our courts have done. And this brings me to the consideration of American courts as legislative chambers.

CHAPTER III

AMERICAN COURTS AS LEGISLATIVE CHAMBERS

In one point of view many of the greatest of the Federalists were idealists. They seem sincerely to have believed that they could, by some form of written words, constrain a people to be honest against their will, and almost as soon as the new government went into operation they tested these beliefs by experiment, with very indifferent success. I take it that jurists like Jay and Marshall held it to be axiomatic that rules of conduct should be laid down by them which would be applicable to rich and poor, great and small, alike, and that courts could maintain such rules against all pressure. Possibly such principles may be enforced against individuals, but they cannot be enforced against communities, and it was here that the Federalist philosophy collapsed, as Hamilton, at least partly, foresaw that it must.

Sovereigns have always enjoyed immunity

from suit by private persons, unless they have been pleased to assent thereto, not because it is less wrongful for a sovereign than for an individual to cheat, but because the sovereign cannot be arrested and the individual can. With the Declaration of Independence the thirteen colonies became sovereigns. Petty sovereigns it is true, and singly contemptible in physical force as against most foreign nations, but none the less tenacious of the attributes of sovereignty, and especially of the attribute which enabled them to repudiate their debts. Jay, Marshall, and their like, thought that they could impose the same moral standard upon the states as upon private persons; they were unable to do so, but in making the attempt they involved the American judicial system in a maze of difficulties whose gravity, I fear, can hardly be exaggerated. Before entering upon this history, however, I must say a word touching the nature of our law.

Municipal law, to be satisfactory, should be a body of abstract principles capable of being applied impartially to all relevant facts, just as Marshall and Jay held it to be. Where exceptions begin, equality before the law ends, as I have tried to show by the story of King David and Uriah, and therefore the great effort of civilization has been to remove judges from the possibility of being subjected to a temptation, or to a pressure, which may deflect them from impartiality as between suitors. In modern civilization, especially, nothing is so fatal to the principle of order as inequality in the dispensation of justice, and it would have been reasonable to suppose that Americans, beyond all others, would have been alive to this teaching of experience, and have studiously withdrawn their bench from politics. In fact they have ignored it, and instead they have set their judiciary at the focus of conflicting forces. The result has been the more unfortunate as the English system of jurisprudence is ill calculated to bear the strain, it being inflexible. In theory the English law moves logically from precedent to precedent, the judge originating nothing, only elaborating ideas which he has received from a predecessor, and which are binding on him. If the line of precedents leads to wrongful conclusions, the legislature must intervene with a statute rectifying the wrong. The Romans, who were gifted with a higher legal genius than we, managed better. The prætor, by his edict, suppressed inconvenient precedents, and hence the Romans maintained flexibility in their municipal law without falling into confusion. We have nothing to correspond to the prætor.

Thus the English system of binding precedents is troublesome enough in a civilization in chronic and violent flux like modern civilization, even when applied to ordinary municipal law which may be changed at will by legislation, but it brings society almost to a stand when applied to the most vital functions of government, with no means at hand to obtain a corrective. For the court of last resort having once declared the meaning of a clause of the Constitution, that meaning remains fixed forever, unless the court either reverses itself, which is a disaster, or the Constitution can be amended by the states, which is not only difficult, but which, even if it be possible, entails years of delay.

Yet pressing emergencies arise, emergencies in which a settlement of some kind must almost necessarily be reached somewhat rapidly to avert very serious disorders, and it has been under this tension, as I understand American constitutional development, that our courts have resorted to legislation. Nor is it fair for us to measure the sagacity of our great jurists by the standard of modern experience. They lived before the acceleration of movement by electricity and steam. They could not foresee the rapidity and the profundity of the changes which were imminent. Hence it was that, in the spirit of great lawyers, who were also possibly men tinged with a certain enthusiasm for the ideal, they began their work by ruling on the powers and limitations of sovereignty, as if they were ruling on the necessity of honest intent in dealings with one's neighbor.

In 1789 General Washington is said to have offered John Jay his choice of offices under the new government, and Jay chose the chief justiceship, because there he thought he could make his influence felt most widely. If so he had his wish, and very shortly met with disappointment. In the August Term of 1792, one Chisholm, a citizen of South Carolina, sued the State of Georgia for a debt. Georgia declined to appear, and in February, 1793, Jay, in an elaborate opinion, gave judgment for Chisholm. Jay was followed by his associates with the exception of Iredell, J., of

North Carolina. Forthwith a ferment began, and in the very next session of Congress an amendment to the Constitution was proposed to make such suits impossible. In January, 1798, five years after the case was argued, this amendment was declared to be adopted, but meanwhile Jay had resigned to become governor of New York. In December, 1800, he was again offered the chief justiceship by John Adams, on the resignation of Oliver Ellsworth, but Jay resolutely declined. I have often wondered whether Jay's mortification at having his only important constitutional decision summarily condemned by the people may not have given him a distaste for judicial life.

The Federalist attempt to enforce on the states a positive rule of economic morality, therefore, collapsed at once, but it still remained possible to approach the same problem from its negative side, through the clause of the Constitution which forbade any state to impair the validity of contracts, and Marshall took up this aspect of the task where Jay left it. In Marshall's mind his work was simple. He had only to determine the nature of a contract, and the rest followed automatically.

All contracts were to be held sacred. Their greater or less importance was immaterial.

In 1810 Marshall expounded this general principle in Fletcher v. Peck.[1] "When ... a law is in its nature a contract ... a repeal of the law cannot devest" rights which have vested under it. A couple of years later he applied his principle to the extreme case of an unlimited remission of taxation.[2] The State of New Jersey had granted an exemption from taxation to lands ceded to certain Indians. Marshall held that this contract ran with the land, and inured to the benefit of grantees from the Indians. If the state cared to resume its power of taxation, it must buy the grant back, and the citizens of New Jersey must pay for their improvidence.

Seven years later, in 1819, Marshall may, perhaps, be said to have reached the culmination of his career, for then he carried his moral standard to a breaking strain. But, though his theory broke down, perhaps the most striking evidence of his wonderful intellectual superiority is that he convinced the Democrat, Joseph Story, — a man

[1] 6 Cranch 135.
[2] New Jersey v. Wilson, 7 Cranch 164, decided in 1812.

who had been nominated by Madison to oppose him, and of undoubted strength of character, — of the soundness of his thesis. In 1769 King George III incorporated certain Trustees of Dartmouth College. The charter was accepted and both real and personal property were thereupon conveyed to this corporate body, in trust for educational purposes. In 1816 the legislature of New Hampshire reorganized the board of trustees against their will. If the incorporation amounted to a contract, the Court was clear that this statute impaired it; therefore the only really debatable issue was whether the grant of a charter by the king amounted to a contract by him, with his subjects to whom he granted it. After prolonged consideration Marshall concluded that it did, and I conceive that, in the eye of history, he was right. Throughout the Middle Ages corporate privileges of all kinds, but especially municipal corporate privileges, had been subjects of purchase and sale, and indeed the mediæval social system rested on such contracts. So much was this the case that the right to return members of Parliament from incorporated boroughs was, as Lord Eldon pointed out in the debates on the

Reform Bill, as much private property "as any of your lordships'" titles and peerages.

It was here that Marshall faltered. He felt that the public would not support him if he held that states could not alter town and county charters, so he arbitrarily split corporations in halves, protecting only those which handled exclusively private funds, and abandoning "instruments of government," as he called them, to the mercy of legislative assemblies.

Toward 1832 it became convenient for middle class Englishmen to confiscate most of the property which the aristocracy had invested in parliamentary boroughs, and this social revolution was effected without straining the judicial system, because of the supremacy of Parliament. In America, at about the same time, it became, in like manner, convenient to confiscate numerous equally well-vested rights, because, to have compensated the owners would have entailed a considerable sacrifice which neither the public nor the promoters of new enterprises were willing to make. The same end was reached in America as in England, in spite of Chief Justice Marshall and the Dartmouth College Case, only in America it was attained by a legal somerset which has disordered the course of justice ever since.

In 1697 King William III incorporated Trinity Church in the City of New York, confirming to the society the possession of a parcel of land, adjoining the church, to be used as a churchyard for the burial of the dead. In 1823 the government of New York prohibited interments within the city limits, thus closing the churchyard for the purposes for which it had been granted. As compensation was refused, it appeared to be a clear case of confiscation, and Trinity resisted. In the teeth of recent precedents the Supreme Court of New York decided that, under the *Police Power*, the legislature of New York might authorize this sort of appropriation of private property for sanitary purposes, without paying the owners for any loss they might thereby sustain.[1]

The court thus simply dispensed the legislature from obedience to the law, saying in effect, "although the Constitution forbids impairing contracts, and although this is a contract which you have impaired, yet, in our discretion, we suspend the operation of the Constitution, in this instance,

[1] Coates *v.* Mayor of New York, 7 Cowen 585.

by calling your act an exercise of a power unknown to the framers of the Constitution." I cannot doubt that Marshall would have flouted this theory had he lived to pass upon it, but Marshall died in 1835, and the Charles River Bridge Case, in which this question was first presented to the Supreme Court of the United States, did not come up until 1837. Then Joseph Story, who remained as the representative of Marshall's philosophy upon the bench, vehemently protested against the latitudinarianism of Chief Justice Taney and his associates, but without producing the slightest effect.

In 1785 the Massachusetts legislature chartered the Charles River Bridge Company to build a bridge between Boston and Charlestown, authorizing it, by way of consideration, to collect tolls for forty years. In 1792 the franchise was extended to seventy years, when the bridge was to revert to the Commonwealth. In 1828 the legislature chartered the Warren Bridge Company, expressly to build a bridge parallel to and practically adjoining the Charles River Bridge, the Warren Bridge to become a free bridge after six years. The purpose, of course, was to accelerate movement by ruining the Charles River Bridge Company.

The Charles River Bridge Company sought to restrain the building of the Warren Bridge as a breach of contract by the State, but failed to obtain relief in the state courts, and before the cause could be argued at Washington the Warren Bridge had become free and had destroyed the value of the Charles River Bridge, though its franchise had still twenty years to run. As Story pointed out, no one denied that the charter of the Charles River Bridge Company was a contract, and, as he insisted, it is only common sense as well as common justice and elementary law, that contracts of this character should be reasonably interpreted so far as quiet enjoyment of the consideration granted is concerned; but all this availed nothing. The gist of the opposing argument is contained in a single sentence in the opinion of the Chief Justice who spoke for the majority of the court: "The millions of property which have been invested in railroads and canals, upon lines of travel which had been before occupied by turnpike corporations, will be put in jeopardy" if this doctrine is to prevail.[1]

The effect of the adoption by the Supreme

[1] Charles River Bridge v. Warren Bridge, 11 Peters 420, 553.

Court of the United States of the New York theory of the Police Power was to vest in the judiciary, by the use of this catch-word, an almost unparalleled prerogative. They assumed a supreme function which can only be compared to the Dispensing Power claimed by the Stuarts, or to the authority which, according to the Council of Constance, inheres in the Church, to "grant indulgences for reasonable causes." I suppose nothing in modern judicial history has ever resembled this assumption; and yet, when we examine it, we find it to be not only the logical, but the inevitable, effect of those mechanical causes which constrain mankind to move along the lines of least resistance.

Marshall, in a series of decisions, laid down a general principle which had been proved to be sound when applied by ordinary courts, dealing with ordinary social forces, and operating under the corrective power of either a legislature or a prætor, but which had a different aspect under the American constitutional system. He held that the fundamental law, embodied in the Constitution, commanded that all contracts should be sacred. Therefore he, as a judge, had but two questions to resolve: First, whether, in the case before him, a contract had been proved to exist. Second, admitting that a contract had been proved, whether it had also been shown to have been impaired.

Within ten years after these decisions it had been found in practice that public opinion would not sustain so rigid an administration of the law. No legislature could intervene, and a pressure was brought to bear which the judges could not withstand; therefore, the Court yielded, declaring that if impairing a contract were, on the whole, for the public welfare, the Constitution, as Marshall interpreted it, should be suspended in favor of the legislation which impaired it. They called this suspension the operation of the "Police Power." It followed, as the "Police Power" could only come into operation at the discretion of the Court, that, therefore, within the limits of judicial discretion, confiscation, however arbitrary and to whatever extent, might go on. In the energetic language of the Supreme Court of Maine: "This duty and consequent power override all statute or contract exemptions. The state cannot free any person or corporation from subjection to this power. All personal, as well as property rights must be held subject to the Police Power of the state."[1]

Once the theory of the Police Power was established it became desirable to define the limits of judicial discretion, but that proved to be impossible. It could not be determined in advance by abstract reasoning. Hence, as each litigation arose, the judges could follow no rule but the rule of common sense, and the Police Power, translated into plain English, presently came to signify whatever, at the moment, the judges happened to think reasonable. Consequently, they began guessing at the drift of public opinion, as it percolated to them through the medium of their education and prejudices. Sometimes they guessed right and sometimes wrong, and when they guessed wrong they were cast aside, as appeared dramatically enough in the temperance agitation.

Up to about the middle of the last century the lawfulness of the liquor business had been unquestioned in the United States, and money had been invested as freely in it as in any other legiti-

[1] Boston & Maine Railroad *v.* County Commissioners, 79 Maine 393.

mate enterprise; but, as the temperance agitation swept over the country, in obedience to the impulsion given by science to the study of hygiene, dealing in liquor came to be condemned as a crime. Presently legislatures began to pass statutes to confiscate, more or less completely, this kind of property, and sufferers brought their cases before the courts to have the constitutionality of the acts tested, under the provisions which existed in all state constitutions, forbidding the taking, by the public, of private property without compensation, or without due process of law. Such a provision existed in the constitution of the State of New York, adopted in 1846, and it was to invoke the protection of this clause that one Wynehamer, who had been indicted in 1855, carried his case to the Court of Appeals in the year 1856. In that cause Mr. Justice Comstock, who was one of the ablest jurists New York ever produced, gave an opinion which is a model of judicial reasoning. He showed conclusively the absurdity of constitutional restrictions, if due process of law may be held to mean the enactment of the very statute drawn to work confiscation.[1]

[1] Wynehamer v. The People, 13 N.Y. 393.

This decision, which represented the profoundest convictions of men of the calibre of Comstock and Denio, deserves to rank with Marshall's effort in the Dartmouth College Case. In both instances the tribunal exerted itself to carry out Hamilton's principle of judicial duty by exercising its *judgment* and not its *will*. In other words, the judges propounded a general rule and then simply determined whether the set of facts presented to them fell within that rule. They resolutely declined to legislate by entering upon a consideration of the soundness or reasonableness of the policy which underlay the action of the legislature. In the one case as in the other the effort was unavailing, as Jefferson prophesied that it would be. I have told of Marshall's overthrow in the Charles River Bridge Case, and in 1887, after controversies of this category had begun to come before the Supreme Court of the United States under the Fourteenth Amendment, Mr. Justice Harlan swept Mr. Justice Comstock aside by quietly ignoring an argument which was unanswerable.[1] The same series of phenomena have appeared in regard to laws confiscating prop-

[1] Mugler *v.* Kansas, 123 U.S. 623.

erty invested in lotteries, when opinion turned against lotteries, or in occupations supposed to be unsanitary, as in the celebrated case of the taxing out of existence of the rendering establishment which had been erected as a public benefit to relieve the City of Chicago of its offal.[1] In fine, whenever pressure has reached a given intensity, on one pretext or another, courts have enforced or dispensed with constitutional limitations with quite as much facility as have legislatures, and for the same reasons. The only difference has been that the pressure which has operated most directly upon courts has not always been the pressure which has swayed legislatures, though sometimes both influences have combined. For example, during the Civil War, the courts sanctioned everything the popular majority demanded under the pretext of the War Power, as in peace they have sanctioned confiscations for certain popular purposes, under the name of the Police Power. But then, courts have always been sensitive to financial influences, and if they have been flexible in permitting popular confiscation when the path of least resistance has lain that way, they have gone

[1] Fertilizing Co. *v.* Hyde Park, 97 U.S. 659.

quite as far in the reverse direction when the amount of capital threatened has been large enough to be with them a countervailing force.

As the federal Constitution originally contained no restriction upon the states touching the confiscation of the property of their own citizens, provided contracts were not impaired, it was only in 1868, by the passage of the Fourteenth Amendment, that the Supreme Court of the United States acquired the possibility of becoming the censor of state legislation in such matters. Nor did the Supreme Court accept this burden very willingly or in haste. For a number of years it labored to confine its function to defining the limits of the Police Power, guarding itself from the responsibility of passing upon the "reasonableness" with which that power was used. It was only by somewhat slow degrees, as the value of the threatened property grew to be vast, that the Court was deflected from this conservative course into effective legislation. The first prayers for relief came from the Southern states, who were still groaning under reconstruction governments; but as the Southern whites were then rather poor, their complaints were neglected. The first very famous cause of this category is known as the Slaughter House Cases. In 1869 the Carpet Bag government of Louisiana conceived the plan of confiscating most of the property of the butchers who slaughtered for New Orleans, within a district about as large as the State of Rhode Island. The Fourteenth Amendment forbade states to deprive any person of life, liberty, or property, without due process of law, and the butchers of New Orleans prayed for protection, alleging that the manner in which their property had been taken was utterly lawless. But the Supreme Court declined to interfere, explaining that the Fourteenth Amendment had been contrived to protect the emancipated slaves, and not to make the federal judiciary "a perpetual censor upon all legislation of the states, on the civil rights of their own citizens, with authority to nullify such as it did not approve." [1]

Although, even at that relatively early day, this conservatism met with strong opposition within the Court itself, the pressure of vested wealth did not gather enough momentum to overcome the inertia of the bench for nearly another generation.

[1] Slaughter House Cases, 16 Wallace 78, decided in 1873.

It was the concentration of capital in monopoly, and the consequent effort by the public to regulate monopoly prices, which created the stress which changed the legal equilibrium. The modern American monopoly seems first to have generated that amount of friction, which habitually finds vent in a great litigation, about the year 1870; but only some years later did the states enter upon a determined policy of regulating monopoly prices by law, with the establishment by the Illinois legislature of a tariff for the Chicago elevators. The elevator companies resisted, on the ground that regulation of prices in private business was equivalent to confiscation, and so in 1876 the Supreme Court was dragged into this fiercest of controversies, thereby becoming subject to a stress to which no judiciary can safely be exposed. Obviously two questions were presented for adjudication : The first, which by courtesy might be termed legal, was whether the fixing of prices by statute was a prerogative which a state legislature might constitutionally exercise at all; the second, which was purely political, was whether, admitting that, in the abstract, such a power could be exercised by the state, Illinois had, in this particular case, behaved *reasonably*. The Supreme Court made a conscientious effort to adhere to the theory of Hamilton, that it should, in emergencies like this, use its *judgment* only, and not its *will;* that it should lay down a rule, not vote on the wisdom of a policy. So the judges decided that, from time immemorial, the fixing of prices in certain trades and occupations had been a legislative function, which they supposed might be classified as a branch of the Police Power, but they declared that with this expression of opinion their jurisdiction ended. When it came to asking them to criticise the propriety of legislation, it was, in substance, proposing that they should substitute their *will* for the *will* of the representatives of the people, which was impossible. I well remember the stir made by the case of Munn *v.* Illinois.[1]

Both in and out of the legal profession, those in harmony with the great vested interests complained that the Court had shirked its duty. But these complaints soon ceased, for a movement was in progress which swept, for the moment, all before it. The great aggregations of capital,

[1] 94 U.S. 113.

which had been accumulating ever since the Charles River Bridge Case, not long after Munn *v.* Illinois attained to a point at which they began to grasp many important prerogatives of sovereignty, and to impose, what was tantamount to, arbitrary taxation upon a large scale. The crucial trial of strength came on the contest for control of the railways, and in that contest concentrated capital prevailed. The Supreme Court reversed its attitude, and undertook to do that which it had solemnly protested it could not do. It began to censor legislation in the interest of the strongest force for the time being, that force being actually financial. By the year 1890 the railway interest had expanded prodigiously. Between 1876 and 1890 the investment in railways had far more than doubled, and, during the last five years of this period, the increment had been at an average of about $450,000,000 annually. At this point the majority of the court yielded, as ordinary political chambers always must yield, to extraordinary pressure. Mr. Justice Bradley, however, was not an ordinary man. He was, on the contrary, one of the ablest and strongest lawyers who sat on the federal bench during the last half

AMERICAN COURTS AS LEGISLATIVE CHAMBERS 103

of the nineteenth century; and Bradley, like Story before him, remonstrated against turning the bench of masigtrates, to which he belonged, from a tribunal which should propound general rules applicable to all material facts, into a jury to find verdicts on the reasonableness of the votes of representative assemblies. The legislature of Minnesota, in 1887, passed a statute to regulate railway rates, and provided that the findings of the commission which it erected to fix those rates should be final. The Chicago, Milwaukee & St. Paul Railway contended that this statute was unconstitutional, because it was unreasonable, and the majority of the Court sustained their contention.[1] Justices Bradley, Gray, and Lamar dissented, and Bradley on this occasion delivered an opinion, from which I shall quote a paragraph or two, since the argument appears to me conclusive, not only from the point of view of law, but of political expediency and of common sense : —

"I cannot agree to the decision of the court in this case. It practically overrules Munn *v.*

---

[1] Chicago, Milwaukee & St. Paul Ry. *v.* Minnesota, 134 U.S. 461, decided March 24, 1890.

Illinois. . . . The governing principle of those cases was that the regulation and settlement of the fares of railroads and other public accommodations is a legislative prerogative, and not a judicial one. This is a principle which I regard as of great importance. . . .

"But it is said that all charges should be reasonable, and that none but reasonable charges can be exacted; and it is urged that what is a reasonable charge is a judicial question. On the contrary, it is preëminently a legislative one, involving considerations of policy as well as of remuneration. . . . By the decision now made we declare, in effect, that the judiciary, and not the legislature, is the final arbiter in the regulation of fares and freights of railroads. . . . It is an assumption of authority on the part of the judiciary which, . . . it has no right to make. The assertion of jurisdiction by this court makes it the duty of every court of general jurisdiction, state or federal, to entertain complaints [of this nature], for all courts are bound by the Constitution of the United States, the same as we are."

There is little to add to these words. When the Supreme Court thus undertook to determine the reasonableness of legislation it assumed, under a somewhat thin disguise, the position of an upper chamber, which, though it could not originate, could absolutely veto most statutes touching the use or protection of property, for the administration of modern American society now hinges on this doctrine of judicial dispensation under the Police Power. Whether it be a regulation of rates and prices, of hours of labor, of height of buildings, of municipal distribution of charity, of flooding a cranberry bog, or of prescribing to sleeping-car porters duties regarding the lowering of upper berths, — in questions great and small, the courts vote upon the reasonableness of the use of the Police Power, like any old-fashioned town meeting. There is no rule of law involved. There is only opinion or prejudice, or pecuniary interest. The judges admit frankly that this is so. They avow that they try to weigh public opinion, as well as they can, and then vote. In 1911 Mr Justice Holmes first explained that the Police Power extended to all great public needs, and then went on to observe that this Police Power, or extraordinary prerogative, might be put forth by legislatures "in aid of what is sanctioned by usage, or held by . . . preponderant opinion to be . . . necessary to the public welfare." [1]

A representative chamber reaches its conclusions touching "preponderant opinion" by a simple process, but the influences which sway courts are obscurer, — often, probably, beyond the sphere of the consciousness of the judges themselves. Nor is this the worst; for, as I have already explained, the very constitution of a court, if it be a court calculated to do its legitimate work upon a lofty level, precludes it from keeping pace with the movement in science and the arts. Necessarily it lags some years behind. And this tendency, which is a benefit in the dispensation of justice as between private litigants, becomes a menace when courts are involved in politics. A long line of sinister precedents crowd unbidden upon the mind. The Court of King's Bench, when it held Hampden to be liable for the Ship Money, draped the scaffold for Charles I. The Parliament of Paris, when it denounced Turgot's edict touching the corvée, threw wide the gate by which the aristocracy of France passed to the guillotine. The ruling of the Superior Court of

[1] Noble State Bank *v.* Haskell, 219 U.S. 104.

the Province of Massachusetts Bay, in the case of the Writs of Assistance, presaged the American Revolution; and the Dred Scott decision was the prelude to the Civil War.

The capital essential of justice is that, under like conditions, all should fare alike. The magistrate should be no respecter of persons. The vice of our sytem of judicial dispensation is that it discriminates among suitors in proportion to their power of resistance. This is so because, under adequate pressure, our courts yield along the path of least resistance. I should not suppose that any man could calmly turn over the pages of the recent volumes of the reports of the Supreme Court of the United States and not rise from the perusal convinced that the rich and the poor, the strong and the weak, do not receive a common measure of justice before that judgment seat. Disregarding the discrimination which is always apparent against those who are unpopular, or who suffer under special opprobrium, as do liquor dealers, owners of lotteries, and the like,[1] I will take, nearly

---

[1] See the extraordinary case of Douglas v. Kentucky, 168 U.S. 488, which must be read in connection with Gregory v. Trustees of Shelby College, 2 Metc. (Kentucky) 589.

at random, a couple of examples of rate regulation, where tenderness has been shown property in something approaching to a mathematical ratio to the amount involved.

In April, 1894, a record was produced before the Supreme Court which showed that the State of North Dakota had in 1891 established rates for elevating and storing grain, which rates the defendant, named Brass, who owned a small elevator, alleged to be, to him in particular, *utterly* ruinous, and to be in general unreasonable. He averred that he used his elevator for the storage of his own grain, that it cost about $3000, that he had no monopoly, as there were many hundred such elevators in the state, and, as land fit for the purpose of building elevators was plenty and cheap, that any man could build an elevator in the town in which he lived, as well as he; that the rates he charged were reasonable, and that, were he compelled to receive grain generally at the rates fixed by the statute, he could not store his own grain. All these facts were admitted by demurrer, and Brass contended that if any man's property were ever to be held to be appropriated by the public without compensation, and under no form of law at all save a predatory statute, it should be his; but the Supreme Court voted the Dakota statute to be a reasonable exercise of the Police Power,[1] and dismissed Brass to his fate.

The converse case is a very famous one known as Smyth v. Ames,[2] decided four years later, in 1898. In that case it appeared that the State of Nebraska had, in 1893, reduced freight rates within the state about twenty-nine per cent, in order to bring them into some sort of relation to the rates charged in the adjoining State of Iowa, which were calculated to be forty per cent lower than the Nebraska rates. Several of the most opulent and powerful corporations of the Union were affected by this law, among others the exceedingly prosperous and influential Chicago, Burlington & Quincy Railway. No one pretended that, were the law to be enforced, the total revenues of the Burlington would be seriously impaired, nor was it even clear that, were the estimate of reduction, revenue, and cost confined altogether to the commerce carried on within the limits of the State of Nebraska, leaving interstate

---

[1] Brass v. North Dakota, 153 U.S. 391.
[2] 169 U.S. 466.

commerce out of consideration, a loss would be suffered during the following year. Trade might increase with cheaper rates, or economies might be made by the company, or both causes and many others of increased earnings might combine. Corporation counsel, however, argued that, were the principle of the statute admitted, and should all the states through which the line passed do the like, ultimately a point might be reached at which the railway would be unable to maintain, even approximately, its dividend of eight per cent, and that the creation of such a possibility was conceding the power of confiscation, and, therefore, an unreasonable exercise of the Police Power, by the State of Nebraska. With this argument the Supreme Court concurred. They held the Nebraska statute to be unreasonable. Very possibly it may have been unsound legislation, yet it is noteworthy that within three years after this decision Mr. Hill bought the Chicago, Burlington & Quincy, at the rate of $200 for every share of stock of the par value of $100, thus fixing forever, on the community tributary to the road, the burden of paying a revenue on just double the value of all the stock which it had been found necessary to issue to build the highway. Even at this price Mr. Hill is supposed to have made a brilliant bargain.

This brings me to the heart of my theorem. Ever since Hamilton's time, it has been assumed as axiomatic, by conservative Americans, that courts whose function is to expound a written constitution can and do act as a "barrier to the encroachments and oppressions of the representative body."[1] I apprehend that courts can perform no such office and that in assuming attributes beyond the limitations of their being they, as history has abundantly proved, not only fail in their object, but shake the foundations of authority, and immolate themselves. Hitherto I have confined myself to adducing historical evidence to prove that American courts have, as a whole, been gifted with so little political sagacity that their interference with legislation, on behalf of particular suitors, has, in the end, been a danger rather than a protection to those suitors, because of the animosity which it has engendered. I shall now go further. For the sake of argument I am willing to admit that the courts, in the exercise

[1] *The Federalist*, No. LXXVIII.

of the dispensing prerogative, called the Police Power, have always acted wisely, so much so that every such decree which they have issued may be triumphantly defended upon economic, moral, or social grounds. Yet, assuming this to be true, though I think I have shown it to be untrue, the assumption only strengthens my contention, that our courts have ceased to be true courts, and are converted into legislative chambers, thereby promising shortly to become, if they are not already, a menace to order. I take it to be clear that the function of a legislature is to embody the will of the dominant social force, for the time being, in a political policy explained by statutes, and when that policy has reached a certain stage of development, to cause it to be digested, together with the judicial decisions relevant to it, in a code. This process of correlation is the highest triumph of the jurist, and it was by their easy supremacy in this field of thought, that Roman lawyers chiefly showed their preëminence as compared with modern lawyers. Still, while admitting this superiority, it is probably true that the Romans owed much of their success in codification to the greater permanence of the Roman legislative tenure of office, and, therefore, stability of policy,—phenomena which were both probably effects of a slower social movement among the ancients. The Romans, therefore, had less need than we of a permanent judiciary to counteract the disintegrating tendency of redundant legislation; *a fortiori*, of course, they had still less to isolate the judiciary from political onslaughts which might cause justice to become a series of exceptions to general principles, rather than a code of unvarying rules.

It is precisely because they are, and are intended to be, arenas of political combat, that legislatures cannot be trustworthy courts, and it was because this fact was notorious that the founders of this government tried to separate the legislative from the judicial function, and to make this separation the foundation of the new republic. They failed, as I conceive, not because they made their legislatures courts, but because, under the system they devised, their courts have become legislatures. A disease, perhaps, the more insidious of the two. Insidious because it undermines order, while legislative murder and confiscation induce reaction.

If a legislative chamber would act as a court, the first necessity is to eliminate its legislative character. For example, the House of Lords in England has long discharged the duties of a tribunal of last resort for the empire, and with general approbation, but only because, when sitting as a court, the law lords sit alone. Politicians and political influences are excluded. Where political influences enter disaster follows. Hence the infamous renown of political decisions in legal controversies, such as bills of attainder and *ex post facto* laws, or special legislation to satisfy claims which could not be defended before legitimate courts, or the scandals always attending the trial of election petitions. The object of true courts is to shield the public from these and kindred abuses.

In primitive communities courts are erected to defend the weak against the strong, by correlating local customs in such wise that some general principle can be deduced which shall protect the civil rights of those who cannot protect themselves, against the arbitrary exactions of powerful neighbors. In no community can every person have equal civil rights. That is impossible. Civil rights must vary according to status. But such rights as any person may have, those the courts are bound to guard indifferently. If the courts do not perform this, their first and most sacred duty, I apprehend that order cannot be permanently maintained, for this is equality before the law; and equality before the law is the cornerstone of order in every modern state.

I conceive that the lawyers of the age of Washington were the ablest that America has ever produced. No men ever understood the principle of equality before the law more thoroughly than they, and after the establishment of this government a long series of great and upright magistrates strove, as I have shown, to carry this principle into effect. Jay and Marshall, Story and Bradley, and many, many more, struggled, protested, and failed. Failed, as I believe, through no fault of their own, but because fortune had placed them in a position untenable for the judge. When plunged in the vortex of politics, courts must waver as do legislatures, and nothing is to me more painful than to watch the process of deterioration by which our judges lose the instinct which should warn them to shun legislation as a breach of trust, and to cleave to those general principles which permit of no exceptions. To illustrate my meaning I shall refer to but one litigation, but that one is so extraordinary that I must deal with it in detail.

In 1890 the dread of the enhancement of prices by monopoly, as the Supreme Court itself has explained, caused Congress to pass the famous Sherman Act, which prohibited indiscriminately all monopolies or restraints of trade. Presently the government brought a bill to dissolve an obnoxious railway pool, called the Trans-Missouri Freight Association, and in 1896 the case came up for adjudication. I have nothing to say touching the policy involved. I am only concerned with a series of phenomena, developed through several years, as effects of pressure acting upon a judiciary, exposed as the judiciary, under our system, is exposed.

The Trans-Missouri Case was argued on December 8, 1896, very elaborately and by the most eminent counsel. After long consideration, and profound reflection, Mr. Justice Peckham, speaking for the majority of the tribunal, laid down a general principle in conformity to the legislative will, precisely as Marshall had laid down a general principle in the Dartmouth College Case, or Story in the Charles River Bridge Case, or Waite in Munn *v.* Illinois, or Bradley in the Minnesota Rate Case. Then the process of agitation immediately began. In the words of Mr. Justice Harlan, fifteen years later: "But those who were in combinations that were illegal did not despair. They at once set up the baseless claim that the decision of 1896 disturbed the 'business interests of the country,' and let it be known that they would never be content until the rule was established that would permit interstate commerce to be subjected to *reasonable* restraints."[1]

Other great causes, involving the same issue, were tried, the question was repeatedly reargued, but the Supreme Court tenaciously adhered to its general principle, that, under the Sherman Act, *all* restraints of trade, or monopolies, were unlawful, and, therefore, the Court had but two matters before it, first to define a restraint of trade or a monopoly, second to determine whether the particular combination complained of fell within that definition. No discretion was permitted. Judicial duty ended there.

The Court being found to be inflexible, recourse

[1] 221 U.S. 91.

was had to Congress, and a bill in the form of an amendment to the Sherman Act was brought into the Senate authorizing, in substance, those who felt unsafe under the law, to apply to certain government officials, to be permitted to produce evidence of the reasonable methods they employed, and, if the evidence were satisfactory, to receive, what was tantamount to, an indulgence. The subject thus reopened, the Senate Committee on the Judiciary went into the whole question of monopoly anew, and in 1909 Senator Nelson presented an exhaustive report against the proposed relaxation. Thereupon the Senate indefinitely postponed further consideration of the amendment. The chief reasons given by Senator Nelson were summed up in a single sentence: "The defence of reasonable restraint would be made in every case and there would be as many different rules of reasonableness as cases, courts, and juries. . . . To amend the anti-trust act, as suggested by this bill, would be to entirely emasculate it, and for all practical purposes render it nugatory as a remedial statute. . . . The act as it exists is clear, comprehensive, certain and highly remedial. It practically covers the field of federal jurisdiction, and is in every respect a model law. To destroy or undermine it at the present juncture, . . . would be a calamity.

"In view of the foregoing, your committee recommend the indefinite postponement of the bill."[1]

And so the Senate did indefinitely postpone the bill.

Matters stood thus when the government brought process to dissolve the Standard Oil Company, as an unlawful combination. The cause was decided on May 15, 1911, the Chief Justice speaking for the majority of the bench, in one of the most suggestive opinions which I have ever read. To me this opinion, like Taney's opinion in the Charles River Bridge Case, indicates that the tension had reached the breaking point, the court yielding in all directions at once, while the dominant preoccupation of the presiding judge seemed to be to plant his tribunal in such a position that it could so yield, without stultifying itself hopelessly before the legal profession and

---

[1] 60th Congress, 2d Session, Senate, Report No. 848, Adverse Report by Mr. Nelson, Amending Anti-trust Act, January 26, 1909, page 11.

the public. In striving to reach this position, however, I apprehend that the Chief Justice, unreservedly, crossed the chasm on whose brink American jurists had been shuddering for ninety years. The task the Chief Justice assumed was difficult almost beyond precedent. He proposed to surrender to the vested interests the principle of *reasonableness* which they demanded, and which the tribunal he represented, together with Congress, had refused to surrender for fifteen years. To pacify the public, which would certainly resent this surrender, he was prepared to punish two hated corporations, while he strove to preserve, so far as he could, the respect of the legal profession and of the public, for the court over which he presided, by maintaining a semblance of consistency.

To accomplish these contradictory results, the Chief Justice began, rather after the manner of Marshall in Marbury v. Madison, by an extrajudicial disquisition. The object of this disquisition was to justify his admission of the evidence of reasonableness as a defence, although it was not needful to decide that such evidence must be admitted in order to dispose of that particular cause. For the Chief Justice very readily agreed that the Standard Oil Company was, in fact, an unreasonable restraint of trade, and must be dissolved, no matter whether it were allowed to prove its reasonable methods or not. Accordingly, he might have contented himself with stating that, admitting for the sake of argument but without approving, all the defendant advanced, he should sustain the government; but to have so disposed of the case would not have suited his purpose. What the Chief Justice had it at heart to do was to surrender a fundamental principle, and yet to appear to make no surrender at all. Hence, he prepared his preliminary and extra-judicial essay on the human reason, of whose precise meaning, I must admit, I still, after many perusals, have grave doubts. I sometimes suspect that the Chief Justice did not wish to be too explicit. So far as I comprehend the Chief Justice, his chain of reasoning amounted to something like this: It was true, he observed, that for fifteen years the Supreme Court had rejected the evidence of reasonableness which he admitted, and had insisted upon a general principle which he might be supposed to renounce, but this apparent discrepancy involved no contradiction. It was only a progression in thought. For, he continued, the judges who, on various previous occasions, sustained that general principle, must have reached their conclusions by the light of reason; to-day we reach a contrary conclusion, but we also do so by the light of reason; therefore, as all these decisions are guided by the light of reason they fundamentally coincide, however much superficially they may seem to differ.[1]

I have never supposed that this argument carried complete conviction either to the legal profession, to the public, or to Congress. Certainly, it did not convince Mr. Justice Harlan, who failed to fathom it, and bluntly expressed his astonishment in a dissenting opinion in another cause from which I regret to say I can only quote a couple of paragraphs, although the whole deserves attentive perusal: —

"If I do not misapprehend the opinion just delivered, the Court insists that what was said in the opinion in the Standard Oil Case, was in accordance with our previous decisions in the Trans-Missouri and Joint Traffic Cases, . . . if we resort to *reason*. This statement surprises me

[1] Standard Oil Company *v.* United States, 221 U.S. 1.

AMERICAN COURTS AS LEGISLATIVE CHAMBERS 123

quite as much as would a statement that black was white or white was black."

"But now the Court, in accordance with what it denominates the 'rule of reason,' in effect inserts in the act the word 'undue,' which means the same as 'unreasonable,' and thereby makes Congress say what it did not say. . . . And what, since the passage of the act, it has explicitly refused to say. . . . In short, the Court now, by judicial legislation, in effect, amends an Act of Congress relating to a subject over which that department of the Government has exclusive cognizance." [1]

The phenomenon which amazed Mr. Justice Harlan is, I conceive, perfectly comprehensible, if we reflect a little on the conflict of forces involved, and on the path of least resistance open to an American judge seeking to find for this conflict, a resultant. The regulation or the domination of monopoly was an issue going to the foundation of society, and popular and financial energy had come into violent impact in regard to the control of prices. Popular energy found vent through

[1] United States v. American Tobacco Company, 221 U.S. 191, 192.

Congress, while the financiers, as financiers always have and always will, took shelter behind the courts. Congress, in 1890, passed a statute to constrain monopolies, against which financiers protested as being a species of confiscation, and which the Chief Justice himself thought harsh. To this statute the Supreme Court gave a harsh construction, as the Chief Justice had more than once pointed out, when he was still an associate upon the bench. From a series of these decisions an appeal had been made to Congress, and the Senate, in the report from which I have quoted, had sustained the construction given to the statute by the majority of his brethren with whom the Chief Justice differed. Since the last of these decisions, however, the complexion of the bench had been considerably changed by new appointments, much as it had been after Hepburn v. Griswold, and an opportunity seemed to be presented to conciliate every one.

In any other country than the United States, a chief justice so situated would doubtless have affirmed the old precedents, permitting himself, at most, to point out the mischief which, he thought, they worked. Not so a lawyer nurtured under the American constitutional system, which breeds in the judge the conviction that he is superior to the legislator. His instinct, under adequate pressure, is always to overrule anything repugnant to him that a legitimate legislative assembly may have done. In this instance, had the case been one of first impression, nothing would have been easier than to have nullified the Sherman Act as an unreasonable exercise of the Police Power, as judges had been nullifying statutes of which they disapproved for a couple of generations previously; but the case was not one of first impression. On the contrary, the constitutionality of the Sherman Act had been so often upheld by the judiciary that the Chief Justice himself admitted that so long as Congress allowed him to use his reason, these "contentions [were] plainly foreclosed." Therefore, for him the path of least resistance was to use his *reason*, and, as a magistrate, to amend a statute which Congress ought to have amended, but had *unreasonably* omitted to amend. Such was the final and logical result of the blending of judicial and legislative functions in a court, as they are blended under the American constitutional system.

Nor is it unworthy of remark that the Chief Justice, in abstaining from questioning the constitutionality of the act, expressly intimated that he did so because, by the use of his reason, he could make that reasonable and constitutional which otherwise might be unreasonable and unconstitutional. The defendants pressed the argument that destroying the freedom of contract, as the Sherman Law destroyed it, was to infringe upon the "constitutional guaranty of due process of law." To this the Chief Justice rejoined: "But the ultimate foundation of all these arguments is the assumption that reason may not be resorted to in interpreting and applying the statute. . . . As the premise is demonstrated to be unsound by the construction we have given the statute," these arguments need no further notice.[1]

Should Congress amend the Sherman Act, as it seems somewhat disposed to do, by explicitly enacting the rule of the Trans-Missouri Case, a grave issue would be presented. The Chief Justice might submit, and thus avert, temporarily at least, a clash; or, he might hold such an amendment unconstitutional as denying to the Court

[1] 221 U.S. 69.

the right to administer the law according to due process. A trial of strength would then be imminent.

Nearly a century ago, Jefferson wrote to Spencer Roane, "The Constitution, on this hypothesis, is a mere thing of wax in the hands of the judiciary, which they may twist and shape into any form they please." [1] And however much we may recoil from admitting Jefferson's conclusion to be true, it none the less remains the fact that it has proved itself to be true, and that the people have recognized it to be true, and have taken measures to protect themselves by bringing the judiciary under the same degree of control which they enforce on other legislators. The progression has been steady and uniform, each advance toward an assumption of the legislative function by the judiciary having been counterbalanced by a corresponding extension of authority over the courts by the people. First came the protest against Marbury and Madison in the impeachment of Chase, because, as Giles explained, if judges were to annul laws, the dominant party must have on the bench judges they

[1] To Spencer Roane, Sept. 6, 1819, Ford, 10, 141.

could trust. Next the Supreme Court of New York imagined the theory of the Police Power, which was adopted by the Supreme Court of the United States in 1837. But it stood to reason that if judges were to suspend constitutional limitations according to their notions of reasonableness, the people must have the means of securing judges whose views touching reasonableness coincided with their own. And behold, within ten years, by the constitution of 1846, New York adopted an elective judiciary.

Then followed the Dred Scott Case, the Civil War, and the attack on legislative authority in Hepburn *v.* Griswold. Straightway the Court received an admonition which it remembered for a generation. Somewhat forgetful of this, on May 15, 1911, Chief Justice White gave his opinion in the Standard Oil Case, which followed hard upon a number of state decisions intended to override legislation upon several burning social issues. Forthwith, in 1912, the proposition to submit all decisions involving a question of constitutional law to a popular vote became an issue in a presidential election. Only one step farther could be taken, and that we see being taken all about us. Experience has shown, in New York and elsewhere, that an election, even for a somewhat short term, does not bring the judge so immediately under popular control that decisions objectionable to the majority may not be made. Hence the recall. The degradation of the judicial function can, in theory at least, go no farther. Thus the state courts may be said already to be prostrate, or likely shortly to become prostrate. The United States courts alone remain, and, should there be a struggle between them and Congress, the result can hardly be doubted. An event has recently occurred abroad which we may do well to ponder.

Among European nations England has long represented intelligent conservatism, and at the heart of her conservatism lay the House of Lords. Through many centuries and under many vicissitudes this ancient chamber had performed functions of the highest moment, until of late it had come to occupy a position not dissimilar to that which the Supreme Court of the United States yet holds. On one side it was the highest legal tribunal of the Empire, on the other it was a non-representative assembly, seldom indeed originating important legislation, but enjoying an absolute veto on legislation sent it from the Commons. One day in a moment of heated controversy the Lords vetoed a bill on which the Commons had determined. A dissolution followed and the House of Lords, as a political power, faded into a shadow; yet, notwithstanding this, its preëminence as a court has remained intact. Were a similar clash to occur in America no such result could be anticipated. Supposing a President, supported by a congressional majority, were to formulate some policy no more subversive than that which has been formulated by the present British Cabinet, and this policy were to be resisted, as it surely would be, by potent financial interests, the conflicting forces would converge upon the Supreme Court. The courts are always believed to tend toward conservatism, therefore they are generally supported by the conservative interest, both here and elsewhere. In this case a dilemma would be presented. Either the judges would seek to give expression to "preponderant" popular opinion, or they would legislate. In the one event they would be worthless as a restraining influence. In the other, I apprehend, a blow would fall similar to the blow which fell upon the House of Lords, only it would cut deeper. Shearing the House of Lords of political power did not dislocate the administration of English justice, because the law lords are exclusively judges. They never legislate. Therefore no one denounced them. Not even the wildest radical demanded that their tenure should be made elective, much less that they should be subjected to the recall. With us an entirely different problem would be presented for solution. A tribunal, nominally judicial, would throw itself across the path of the national movement. It would undertake to correct a disturbance of the social equilibrium. But what a shifting of the social equilibrium means, and what follows upon tampering with it, is a subject which demands a chapter by itself.

CHAPTER IV

THE SOCIAL EQUILIBRIUM

I ASSUME it as self-evident that those who, at any given moment, are the strongest in any civilization, will be those who are at once the ruling class, those who own most property, and those who have most influence on legislation. The weaker will fare hardly in proportion to their weakness. Such is the order of nature. But, since those are the strongest through whom nature finds it, for the time being, easiest to vent her energy, and as the whole universe is in ceaseless change, it follows that the composition of ruling classes is never constant, but shifts to correspond with the shifting environment. When this movement is so rapid that men cannot adapt themselves to it, we call the phenomenon a revolution, and it is with revolutions that I now have to do.

Nothing is more certain than that the intellectual adaptability of the individual man is very limited. A ruling class is seldom conscious of its own decay, and most of the worst catastrophes of history have been caused by an obstinate resistance to change when resistance was no longer possible. Thus while an incessant alteration in social equilibrium is inevitable, a revolution is a problem in dynamics, on the correct solution of which the fortunes of a declining class depend.

For example, the modern English landlords replaced the military feudal aristocracy during the sixteenth century, because the landlords had more economic capacity and less credulity. The men who supplanted the mediæval soldiers in Great Britain had no scruple about robbing the clergy of their land, and because of this quality they prospered greatly. Ultimately the landlords reached high fortune by controlling the boroughs which had, in the Middle Ages, acquired the right to return members to the House of Commons. Their domination lasted long; nevertheless, about 1760, the rising tide of the Industrial Revolution brought forward another type of mind. Flushed by success in the Napoleonic wars the Tories failed to appreciate that the social equilibrium, by the year 1830, had shifted, and that they no longer commanded enough physical force to maintain their parliamentary ascendancy. They thought they had only to be arrogant to prevail, and so they put forward the Duke of Wellington as their champion. They could hardly have made a poorer choice. As Disraeli has very truly said, "His Grace precipitated a revolution which might have been delayed for half a century, and need never have occurred in so aggravated a form." The Duke, though a great general, lacked knowledge of England. He began by dismissing William Huskisson from his Cabinet, who was not only its ablest member, but perhaps the single man among the Tories who thoroughly comprehended the industrial age. Huskisson's issue was that the franchise of the intolerably corrupt East Retford should be given to Leeds or Manchester. Having got rid of Huskisson, the Duke declared imperiously that he would concede nothing to the disfranchised industrial magnates, nor to the vast cities in which they lived. A dissolution of Parliament followed and in the election the Tories were defeated. Although Wellington may not have been a sagacious statesman, he was a capable soldier and he knew when he could and when he could not physically fight. On this occasion, to again quote Disraeli, "He rather fled than retired." He induced his friends to absent themselves from the House of Lords and permit the Reform Bill to become law. Thus the English Tories, by their experiment with the Duke of Wellington, lost their boroughs and with them their political preëminence, but at least they saved themselves, their families, and the rest of their property. As a class they have survived to this day, although shorn of much of the influence which they might very probably have retained had they solved more correctly the problem of 1830. In sum, they were not altogether impervious to the exigencies of their environment. The French Revolution is the classic example of the annihilation of a rigid organism, and it is an example the more worthy of our attention as it throws into terrible relief the process by which an intellectually inflexible race may convert the courts of law which should protect their decline into the most awful engine for their destruction.

The essence of feudalism was a gradation of rank, in the nature of caste, based upon fear. The clergy were privileged because the laity believed that they could work miracles, and could dispense something more vital even than life and death. The nobility were privileged because they were resistless in war. Therefore, the nobility could impose all sorts of burdens upon those who were unarmed. During the interval in which society centralized and acquired more and more a modern economic form, the discrepancies in status remained, while commensurately the physical or imaginative force which had once sustained inequality declined, until the social equilibrium grew to be extremely unstable. Add to this that France, under the monarchy, was ill consolidated. The provinces and towns retained the administrative complexity of an archaic age, even to local tariffs. Thus under the monarchy privilege and inequality pervaded every phase of life, and, as the judiciary must be, more or less, the mouthpiece of society, the judiciary came to be the incarnation of caste.

Speaking broadly, the judicial office, under the monarchy, was vendible. In legal language, it was an incorporeal hereditament. It could be bought and sold and inherited like an advowson, or right to dispose of a cure of souls in the English

Church, or of a commission in the English army. The system was well recognized and widespread in the eighteenth century, and worked fairly well with the French judiciary for about three hundred years, but it was not adapted to an industrial environment. The judicial career came to be pretty strongly hereditary in a few families, and though the members of these families were, on the whole, self-respecting, honest, and learned, they held office in their own right and not as a public trust. So in England members of the House of Commons, who sat for nomination boroughs, did not, either in fact or theory, represent the inhabitants of those boroughs, but patrons; and in like manner French judges could never learn to regard themselves as the trustees of the civil rights of a nation, but as a component part of a class who held a status by private title. Looked at as a problem in dynamics the inherent vice in all this kind of property and in all this administrative system, was the decay, after 1760, of the physical force which had engendered it and defended it. As in England the ascendancy of the landlords passed away when England turned from an agricultural into an industrial society, so in France priests and nobles fell into contempt, when most peasants knew that the Church could neither harm by its curse nor aid by its blessing, and when commissions in the army were given to children or favorites, as a sort of pension, while the pith of the nation was excluded from military command because it could not prove four quarterings of nobility. Hardly an aristocrat in France had shown military talent for a generation, while, when the revolution began, men like Jourdan and Kleber, Ney and Augereau, and a host of other future marshals and generals had been dismissed from the army, or were eating out their hearts as petty officers with no hope of advancement. Local privileges and inequalities were as intolerable as personal. There were privileged provinces and those administered arbitrarily by the Crown, there were a multiplicity of internal tariffs, and endless municipal franchises and monopolies, so much so that economists estimated that, through artificial restraints, one-quarter of the soil of France lay waste. Turgot, in his edict on the grain trade, explained that kings in the past by ordinance, or the police without royal authority, had compiled a body "of legislation equivalent to a prohibition of bringing grain into Paris," and this condition was universal. One province might be starving and another oppressed with abundance.

Meanwhile, under the stimulant of applied science, centralization went on resistlessly, and the cost of administration is proportionate to centralization. To bear the burden of a centralized government taxes must be equal and movement free, but here was a rapidly centralizing nation, the essence of whose organism was that taxes should be unequal and that movement should be restricted.

As the third quarter of the eighteenth century closed with the death of Louis XV, all intelligent French administrators recognized the dilemma; either relief must be given, or France must become insolvent, and revolution supervene upon insolvency. But for the aristocracy revolution had no terrors, for they believed that they could crush revolution as their class had done for a thousand years.

Robert Turgot was born in 1727, of a respectable family. His father educated him for the Church, but lack of faith caused him to prefer the magistracy, and on the death of his father he obtained a small place in the Court of Parliament. Afterward he became a Master of Requests, and served for seven years in that judicial position, before he was made Intendant of the Province of Limousin. Even thus early in life Turgot showed political sagacity. In an address at the Sorbonne he supported the thesis that "well-timed reform alone averts revolution." Distinguishing himself as Intendant, on the death of Louis XV the King called Turgot to the Council of State, and in August, 1774, Turgot became Minister of Finance. He came in pledged to reform, and by January, 1776, he had formulated his plan. In that month he presented to the King his memorable Six Edicts, the first of which was the most celebrated state paper he ever wrote. It was the Edict for the Suppression of the Corvée. The corvée threw the burden of maintaining the highways on the peasantry by exacting forced labor. It was admittedly the most hateful, the most burdensome, and the most wasteful of all the bad taxes of the time, and Turgot, following the precedent of the Roman Empire, advised instead a general highway impost. The proposed impost in itself was not considerable, and would not have been extraordinarily obnoxious to the privileged classes, but for the principle of equality by which Turgot justified it: "The expenses of government having for their object the interests of all, all should contribute to them; and the more advantages a man has, the more that man should contribute."

Nor was this the most levelling of Turgot's arguments. He pointed out that though originally the exemption from taxation, which the nobility enjoyed, might have been defended on the ground that the nobles were bound to yield military service without pay, such service had long ceased to be performed, while on the contrary titles could be bought for money. Hence every wealthy man became a noble when he pleased, and thus exemption from taxation had come to present the line of cleavage between the rich and poor. By this thrust the privileged classes felt themselves wounded in their vitals, and the Parliament of Paris, the essence of privilege, assumed their defence. To be binding, the edicts had to be registered by the Parliament among the laws of France, and Parliament declined to make registration on the ground that the edicts were unconstitutional, as subversive of the monarchy and of the principle of order. The opinion of the court was long, but a single paragraph gives its purport: "The first rule of justice is to preserve to every one what belongs to him: this rule consists, not only in preserving the rights of property, but still more in preserving those belonging to the person, which arise from the prerogative of birth and of position. . . . From this rule of law and equity it follows that every system which, under an appearance of humanity and beneficence, would tend to establish between men an equality of duties, and to destroy necessary distinctions, would soon lead to disorder (the inevitable result of equality), and would bring about the overturn of civil society."

This judicial opinion was an enunciation of the archaic law of caste as opposed to the modern law of equality, and the cataclysm of the French Revolution hinged upon the incapacity of the French aristocracy to understand that the environment, which had once made caste a necessity, had yielded to another which made caste an impossibility. In vain Turgot and his contemporaries of the industrial type, represented in England by Adam Smith or even by the younger Pitt, explained that unless taxes were equalized and movement accelerated, insolvency must supervene, and that a violent readjustment must follow upon insolvency. With their eyes open to the consequences, the Nobility and Clergy elected to risk revolt, because they did not believe that revolt could prevail against them. Nothing is so impressive in the mighty convulsion which ensued as the mental opacity of the privileged orders, which caused them to increase their pressure in proportion as resistance increased, until finally those who were destined to replace them reorganized the courts, that they might have an instrument wherewith to slaughter a whole race down to the women and children. No less drastic method would serve to temper the rigidity of the aristocratic mind. The phenomenon well repays an hour of study.

Insolvency came within a decade after Turgot's fall, as Turgot had demonstrated that it must come, and an insolvency immediately precipitated by the rapacity of the court which had most need of caution. The future Louis XVIII, for example, who was then known as the Comte de Provence, on one occasion, when the government had made a loan, appropriated a quarter of it, laughingly observing, "When I see others hold out their hands, I hold out my hat." In 1787 the need for money became imperative, and, not daring to appeal to the nation, the King convoked an assembly of "notables," that is to say of the privileged. Calonne, the minister, proposed pretty much the measures of Turgot, and some of these measures the "notables" accepted, but the Parliament of Paris again intervened and declined to register the laws. The Provincial Parliaments followed the Parliament of Paris. After this the King had no alternative but to try the experiment of calling the States-General. They met on May 4, 1789, and instantly an administrative system, which no longer rested upon a social centre of gravity, crumbled, carrying the judiciary with it.

At first the three estates sat separately. If this usage had continued, the Clergy and the Nobles combined would have annulled every measure voted by the Commons. For six weeks the Commons waited. Then on June 10, the Abbé Sieyès said, "Let us cut the cable. It is time." So the Clergy and the Nobility were summoned, and some of the Clergy obeyed. This sufficed. On motion of Sieyès, the Commons proclaimed themselves the National Assembly, and the orders fused. Immediately caste admitted defeat and through its mouthpiece, the King, commanded the Assembly to dissolve. The Commons refused to dissolve, and the Nobles prepared for a *coup d'état*. The foreign regiments, in the pay of the government, were stationed about Paris, while the Bastille, which was supposed to be impregnable, was garrisoned with Swiss. In reply, on July 14, 1789, the citizens of Paris stormed the Bastille. An unstable social equilibrium had been already converted by pressure into a revolution. Nevertheless, excentric as the centre of gravity had now become, it might have been measurably readjusted had the privileged classes been able to reason correctly from premise to conclusion. Men like Lafayette and Mirabeau still controlled the Assembly, and if the King and the Nobility had made terms, probably the monarchy might have been saved, certainly the massacres would have been averted. As a decaying class is apt to do, the Nobility did that which was worst for themselves. Becoming at length partly conscious of a lack of physical force in France to crush the revolution, a portion of the nobility, led by the Comte d'Artois, the future Charles X, fled to Germany to seek for help abroad, while the bolder remained to plan an attack on the rebellion. On October 1, 1789, a great military banquet was given at Versailles. The King and Queen with the Dauphin were present. A royalist demonstration began. The bugles sounded a charge, the officers drew their swords, and the ladies of the court tore the tri-color from the soldiers' coats and replaced it with the white cockade. On October 5, a vast multitude poured out of Paris, and marched to Versailles. The next day they broke into the palace, killed the guards, and carried the King and Queen captive to the Tuileries. But Louis was so intellectually limited that he could not keep faith with those who wished him well. On July 14, 1790, the King swore, before half a million spectators, to maintain the new constitution. In that summer he was plotting to escape to Metz and join the army which had been collected there under the Marquis de Bouillé, while Bouillé himself, after the rising at Nancy, was busy in improving discipline by breaking on the wheel a selection of the soldiers of the Swiss regiment of Châteauvieux which had refused to march against Paris on the 14th of July, 1789. In October, 1790, Louis wrote to the King of Spain and other sovereigns to pay no heed to his concessions for he only yielded to duress, and all this even as Mirabeau made his supreme effort to save those who were fixed upon destroying themselves. Mirabeau sought the King and offered his services. The court sneered at him as a dupe. The Queen wrote, "We make use of Mirabeau, but we do not take him seriously." When Mirabeau awoke to his predicament, he broke out in mixed wrath and scorn: "Of what are these people thinking? Do they not see the abyss yawning at their feet? Both the King and Queen will perish, and you will live to see the rabble spurn their corpses."

The King and Queen, the Nobility and Clergy, could not see the abyss which Mirabeau saw, any more than the lawyers could see it, because of the temper of their minds. In the eye of caste Europe was not primarily divided into nations to whom allegiance was due, but into superimposed orders. He who betrayed his order committed the unpardonable crime. Death were better than that. But to the true aristocrat it was inconceivable that serfs could ever vanquish nobles in battle. Battle must be the final test, and the whole aristocracy of Europe was certain, Frenchmen knew, to succor the French aristocracy in distress.

So in the winter of 1790 the French fugitives congregated at Coblentz on the German frontier, persuaded that they were performing a patriotic duty in organizing an invasion of their country even should their onset be fatal to their relatives and to their King. And Louis doubted not that he also did his duty as a trustee of a divine commission when he in one month swore, before the Assembly, to maintain the constitution tendered him, and in the next authorized his brother, the Comte d'Artois, to make the best combination he could among his brother sovereigns for the gathering of an army to assert his divine prerogative. On June 21, 1791, Louis fled, with his whole family, to join the army of Bouillé, with intent to destroy the entire race of traitors from Mirabeau and Lafayette down to the peasants.

He managed so ill that he was arrested at Varennes, and brought back whence he came, but he lied and plotted still.

Two years had elapsed between the meeting of the States-General and the flight to Varennes, and in that interval nature had been busy in selecting her new favored class. Economists have estimated that the Church owned one-third of the land of Europe during the Middle Ages. However this may have been she certainly held a very large part of France. On April 16, 1790, the Assembly declared this territory to be national property, and proceeded to sell it to the peasantry by means of the paper *assignats* which were issued for the purpose, and were supposed to be secured upon the land. The sales were generally made in little lots, as the sales were made of the public domain in Rome under the Licinian Laws, and with an identical effect. The Emperor of Germany and the King of Prussia met at Pilnitz in August, 1791, to consider the conquest of France, and, on the eve of that meeting, the Assembly received a report which stated that these lands to the value of a thousand million francs had already been distributed, and that sales were going on.

It was from this breed of liberated husbandmen that France drew the soldiers who fought her battles and won her victories for the next five and twenty years.

Assuming that the type of the small French landholder, both rural and urban, had been pretty well developed by the autumn of 1791, the crisis came rapidly, for the confiscations which created this new energy roused to frenzy, perhaps the most formidable energy which opposed it. The Church had not only been robbed of her property but had been wounded in her tenderest part. By a decree of June 12, 1790, the Assembly transferred the allegiance of the French clergy from the Pope to the state, and the priesthood everywhere vowed revenge. In May, 1791, the Marquis de la Rouërie, it is true, journeyed from his home in Brittany to Germany to obtain the recognition of the royal princes for the insurrection which he contemplated in La Vendée, but the insurrection when it occurred was not due so much to him or his kind as to the influence of the nonjuring priests upon the peasant women of the West.

The mental condition of the French emigrants

at Coblentz during this summer of 1791 is nothing short of a psychological marvel. They regarded the Revolution as a jest, and the flight to the Rhine as a picnic. These beggared aristocrats, male and female, would throw their money away by day among the wondering natives, and gamble among themselves at night. If they ever thought of the future it was only as the patricians in Pompey's camp thought; who had no time to prepare for a campaign against Cæsar, because they were absorbed in distributing offices among themselves, or in inventing torments to inflict on the rebels. Their chief anxiety was lest the resistance should be too feeble to permit them to glut themselves with blood. The creatures of caste, the emigrants could not conceive of man as a variable animal, or of the birth of a race of warriors under their eyes. To them human nature remained constant. Such, they believed, was the immutable will of God.

So it came to pass that, as the Revolution took its shape, a vast combination among the antique species came semi-automatically into existence, pledged to envelop and strangle the rising type of man, a combination, however, which only attained to maturity in 1793, after the execution of the King. Leopold II, Emperor of Germany, had hitherto been the chief restraining influence, both at Pilnitz and at Paris, through his correspondence with his sister, Marie Antoinette; but Leopold died on March 1, 1792, and was succeeded by Francis II, a fervid reactionist and an obedient son of the Church. Then caste fused throughout Germany, and Prussia and Austria prepared for war. Rouërie had returned to Brittany and only awaited the first decisive foreign success to stab the Revolution in the back. England also was ripening, and the instinct of caste, incarnated in George III, found its expression through Edmund Burke. In 1790 Burke published his "Reflections," and on May 6, 1791, in a passionate outbreak in the House of Commons, he renounced his friendship with Fox as a traitor to his order and his God. Men of Burke's temperament appreciated intuitively that there could be no peace between the rising civilization and the old, one of the two must destroy the other, and very few of them conceived it to be possible that the enfranchised French peasantry and the small bourgeoisie could endure the shock of all that, in their eyes, was intelligent, sacred, and martial in the world.

Indeed, aristocracy had, perhaps, some justification for arrogance, since the revolt in France fell to its lowest depth of impotence between the meeting at Pilnitz in August, 1791, and the reorganization of the Committee of Public Safety in July, 1793. Until August, 1792, the executive authority remained with the King, but the court of Louis was the focus of resistance to the Revolution, and even though a quasi-prisoner the King was still strong. Monarchy had a firm hold on liberal nobles like Mirabeau and Lafayette, on adventurers like Dumouriez, and even on lawyers like Danton who shrank from excessive cruelty. Had the pure Royalists been capable of enough intellectual flexibility to keep faith upon any reasonable basis of compromise, even as late as 1792, the Revolution might have been benign. In June, 1792, Lafayette, who commanded the army of the North, came to Paris and not only ventured to lecture the Assembly on its duty, but offered to take Louis to his army, who would protect him against the Jacobins. The court laughed at Lafayette as a Don Quixote, and betrayed his plans to the enemy. "I had rather perish," said the Queen, "than be saved by M. de Lafayette and his constitutional friends." And in this she only expressed the conviction which the caste to which she belonged held of their duty. Cazalés protested to the Assembly, "Though the King perish, let us save the kingdom." The Archduchess Christina wrote to her sister, Marie Antoinette, "What though he be slain, if we shall triumph," and Condé, in December, 1790, swore that he would march on Lyons, "come what might to the King."

France was permeated with archaic thought which disorganized the emerging society until it seemingly had no cohesion. To the French emigrant on the Rhine that society appeared like a vile phantom which had but to be exorcised to vanish. And the exorcism to which he had recourse was threats of vengeance, threats which before had terrified, because they had behind them a force which made them good. Torture had been an integral part of the old law. The peasant expected it were he insubordinate. Death alone was held to be too little to inspire respect for caste. Some frightful spectacle was usually provided to magnify authority. Thus Bouillé broke on the wheel, while the men were yet alive, every bone in the bodies of his soldiers when they disobeyed him; and for scratching Louis XV, with a knife, Damiens, after indescribable agonies, was torn asunder by horses in Paris, before an immense multitude. The French emigrants believed that they had only to threaten with a similar fate men like Kellermann and Hoche to make them flee without a blow. What chiefly concerned the nobles, therefore, was not to evolve a masterly campaign, but to propound the fundamental principles of monarchy, and to denounce an awful retribution on insurgents.

By the middle of July, 1792, the Prussians were ready to march, and emperors, kings, and generals were meditating manifestoes. Louis sent the journalist Mallet du Pan to the Duke of Brunswick, the commander-in-chief, to assist him in his task. On July 24, and on August 4, 1792, the King of Prussia laid down the law of caste as emphatically as had the Parliament of Paris some twenty years before. On July 25, the Duke of Brunswick pronounced the doom of the conquered. I come, said the King of Prussia, to prevent the incurable evils which will result to France, to Europe and to all mankind from the spread of the spirit of insubordination, and to this end I shall establish the monarchical power upon a stable basis. For, he continued in the later proclamation, "the supreme authority in France being never ceasing and indivisible, the King could neither be deprived nor voluntarily divest himself of any of the prerogatives of royalty, because he is obliged to transmit them entire with his own crown to his successors."

The Duke of Brunswick's proclamation contained some clauses written expressly for him by Mallet du Pan, and by Limon the Royalist.

If the Palace of the Tuileries be forced, if the least violence be offered to their Majesties, if they are not immediately set at liberty, then will the King of Prussia and the Emperor of Germany inflict "on those who shall deserve it the most exemplary and ever-memorable avenging punishments."

These proclamations reached Paris on July 28, and simultaneously the notorious Fersen wrote the Queen of France, "You have the manifesto, and you should be content."

The court actually believed that, having insulted and betrayed Lafayette and all that body of conservative opinion which might have steadied the social equilibrium, they could rely on the fidelity of regiments filled with men against whom the emigrants and their allies, the Prussians, had just denounced an agonizing death, such as Bouillé's soldiers had undergone, together with the destruction of their homes.

All the world knows what followed. The Royalists had been gathering a garrison for the Tuileries ever since Lafayette's visit, in anticipation of a trial of strength with the Revolutionists. They had brought thither the Swiss guard, fifteen hundred strong; the palace was full of Royalist gentlemen; Mandat, who commanded the National Guard, had been gained over. The approaches were swept by artillery. The court was very confident. On the night of August 9, Mandat was murdered, an insurrectional committee seized the City Hall, and when Louis XVI came forth to review the troops on the morning of the 10th of August, they shouted, "Vive la Nation" and deserted. Then the assault came, the Swiss guard was massacred, the Assembly thrust aside, and the royal family were seized and conveyed to the Temple. There the monarchy ended. Thus far had the irrational opposition of a moribund type thrown into excentricity the social equilibrium of a naturally conservative people. They were destined to drive it still farther.

In this supreme moment, while the Prussians were advancing, France had no stable government and very imperfect means of keeping order. All the fighting men she could muster had marched to the frontier, and, even so, only a demoralized mass of levies, under Dumouriez and Kellermann, lay between the most redoubtable regiments of the world and Paris. The emigrants and the Germans thought the invasion but a military promenade. At home treason to the government hardly cared to hide itself. During much of August the streets of Paris swarmed with Royalists who cursed the Revolution, and with priests more bitter than the Royalists. Under the windows of Louis, as he lay in the Temple, there were cries of "Long live the King," and in the prisons themselves the nobles drank to the allies and corresponded with the Prussians. Finally, Roland, who was minister, so far lost courage that he proposed to withdraw beyond the Loire, but Danton would hear of no retreat. "De l'audace," he cried, "encore de l'audace, et toujours de l'audace."

The Assembly had not been responsible for the assault on the Tuileries on August 10, 1792. Filled with conservatives, it lacked the energy. That movement had been the work of a knot of radicals which had its centre in Danton's Club of the Cordeliers. Under their impulsion the sections of Paris chose commissioners who should take possession of the City Hall and eject the loyalist Council. They did so, and thus Danton became for a season the Minister of Justice and the foremost man in France. Danton was a semi-conservative. His tenure of power was the last possibility of averting the Terror. The Royalists, whom he trusted, themselves betrayed him, and Danton fell, to be succeeded by Robespierre and his political criminal courts. Meanwhile, on September 20, 1792, the Prussian column recoiled before the fire of Kellermann's mob of "vagabonds, cobblers and tailors," on the slope of Valmy, and with the victory of Valmy, the great eighteenth-century readjustment of the social equilibrium of Europe passed into its secondary stage.

CHAPTER V

POLITICAL COURTS

In the eye of philosophy, perhaps the most alluring and yet illusive of all the phenomena presented by civilization is that which we have been considering. Why should a type of mind which has developed the highest prescience when advancing along the curve which has led it to ascendancy, be stricken with fatuity when the summit of the curve is passed, and when a miscalculation touching the velocity of the descent must be destruction?

Although this phenomenon has appeared pretty regularly, at certain intervals, in the development of every modern nation, I conceive its most illuminating example to be that intellectual limitation of caste which, during the French Revolution, led to the creation of those political criminal tribunals which reached perfection with Robespierre.

When coolly examined, at the distance of a

century, the Royalist combination for the suppression of equality before the law, as finally evolved in 1792, did not so much lack military intelligence, as it lacked any approximate comprehension of the modern mind. The Royalists proposed to reëstablish privilege, and to do this they were ready to immolate, if necessary, their King and Queen, and all of their own order who stayed at home to defend them. Indeed, speaking generally, they valued Louis XVI, living, cheaply enough, counting him a more considerable asset if dead. "What a noise it would make throughout Europe," they whispered among themselves, "if the rabble should kill the King."

Nor did Marie Antoinette delude herself on this score. At Pilnitz, in 1791, the German potentates issued a declaration touching France which was too moderate to suit the emigrants, who published upon it a commentary of their own. This commentary was so revolting that when the Queen read her brother-in-law's signature appended to it, she exclaimed — "Cain."

The Royalist plan of campaign was this: They reckoned the energy of the Revolution so low that they counted pretty confidently, in the summer of 1792, on the ability of their party to defend the Tuileries against any force which could be brought against it; but assuming that the Tuileries could not be defended, and that the King and Queen should be massacred, they believed that their own position would be improved. Their monarchical allies would be thereby violently stimulated. It was determined, therefore, that, regardless of consequences to their friends, the invading army should cross the border into Lorraine and, marching by way of Sierk and Rodemach, occupy Châlons. Their entry into Châlons, which they were confident could not be held against them, because of the feeling throughout the country, was to be the signal for the rising in Vendée and Brittany which should sweep down upon Paris from the rear and make the capital untenable. At Châlons the allies would be but ninety miles from Paris, and then nothing would remain but vengeance, and vengeance the more complete the greater the crime had been.

All went well with them up to Valmy. The German advance on August 11, 1792, reached Rodemach, and on August 19, the bulk of the Prussian army crossed the frontier at Rédagne.

On August 20, 1792, Longwy was invested and in three days capitulated. In the camp of the Comte d'Artois "there was not one of us," wrote Las Casas, "who did not see himself, in a fortnight, triumphant, in his own home, surrounded by his humbled and submissive vassals." At length from their bivouacs at Saint-Remy and at Suippes the nobles saw in the distance the towers of Châlons.

The panic at Châlons was so great that orders were given to cut the bridge across the Marne, but it was not until about September 2, that the whole peril was understood at Paris. It is true that for several weeks the government had been aware that the West was agitated and that Rouërie was probably conspiring among the Royalists and nonjuring priests, but they did not appreciate the imminence of the danger. On September 3, at latest, Danton certainly heard the details of the plot from a spy, and it was then, while others quailed, that he incited Paris to audacity. This was Danton's culmination.

As we look back, the weakness of the Germans seems to have been psychological rather than physical. At Valmy the numbers engaged were not unequal, and while the French were, for the most part, raw and ill-compacted levies, with few trained officers, the German regiments were those renowned battalions of Frederick the Great whose onset, during the Seven Years' War, no adversary had been able to endure. Yet these redoubtable Prussians fell back in confusion without having seriously tried the French position, and their officers, apparently, did not venture to call upon them to charge again. In vain the French gentlemen implored the Prussian King to support them if they alone should storm Kellermann's batteries. Under the advice of the Duke of Brunswick the King decided on retreat. It is said that the Duke had as little heart in the war as Charles Fox, or, possibly, Pitt, or as his own troops. And yet he was so strong that Dumouriez, after his victory, hung back and offered the invaders free passage lest the Germans, if aroused, should turn on him and fight their way to the Marne.

To the emigrants the retreat was terrible. It was a disaster from which, as a compact power, they never recovered. The rising in Vendée temporarily collapsed with the check at Châlons, and they were left literally naked unto their enemy. Some of them returned to their homes, preferring the guillotine to starvation, others, disguised in peasants' blouses, tried to reach Rouërie in La Vendée, some died from hardship, some committed suicide, while the bulk regained Liège and there waited as suppliants for assistance from Vienna. But these unfortunate men, who had entered so gayly upon a conflict whose significance they could not comprehend, had by this time lost more than lands and castles. Many of them had lost wives and children in one of the most frightful butcheries of history, and a butchery for which they themselves were responsible, because it was the inevitable and logical effect of their own intellectual limitations.

When, after the affair of August 10, Danton and his party became masters of the incipient republic, Paris lay between two perils whose relative magnitude no one could measure. If Châlons fell, Vendée would rise, and the Republicans of the West would be massacred. Five months later Vendée did rise, and at Machecoul the patriots were slaughtered amidst nameless atrocities, largely at the instigation of the priests. In

March, 1793, one hundred thousand peasants were under arms.

Clearly the West could not be denuded of troops, and yet, if Châlons were to be made good, every available man had to be hurried to Kellermann, and this gigantic effort fell to the lot of a body of young and inexperienced adventurers who formed what could hardly be dignified with the name of an organized administration.

For a long time Marat, with whom Danton had been obliged to coalesce, had been insisting that, if the enemy were to be resisted on the frontier, Paris must first be purged, for Paris swarmed with Royalists wild for revenge, and who were known to be arming. Danton was not yet prepared for extermination. He instituted domiciliary visits. He made about three thousand arrests and seized a quantity of muskets, but he liberated most of those who were under suspicion. The crisis only came with the news, on September 2, of the investment of Verdun, when no one longer could doubt that the net was closing about Paris. Verdun was but three or four days' march from Châlons. When the Duke of Brunswick crossed the Marne and

Brittany revolted, the government would have to flee, as Roland proposed, and then the Royalists would burst the gates of the prisons and there would be another Saint Bartholomew.

Toward four o'clock in the afternoon of September 2, 1792, the prison of the Abbaye was forced and the massacres began. They lasted until September 6, and through a circular sent out by Marat they were extended to Lyons, to Reims, and to other cities. About 1600 prisoners were murdered in Paris alone. Hardly any one has ever defended those slaughters. Even Marat called them "disastrous," and yet no one interfered. Neither Danton, nor Roland, nor the Assembly, nor the National Guard, nor the City of Paris, although the two or three hundred ruffians who did the work could have been dispersed by a single company of resolute men, had society so willed it. When Robespierre's time came he fell almost automatically. Though the head of the despotic "Committee of Public Safety," and nominally the most powerful man in France, he was sent to execution like the vilest and most contemptible of criminals by adversaries who would not command a regiment.

The inference is that the September massacres, which have ever since been stigmatized as the deepest stain upon the Revolution, were, veritably, due to the Royalists, who made with the Republicans an issue of self-preservation. For this was no common war. In Royalist eyes it was a servile revolt, and was to be treated as servile revolts during the Middle Ages had always been treated. Again and again, with all solemnity, the Royalists had declared that were they to return as conquerors no stone of Paris should be left standing on another, and that the inhabitants should expire in the ashes of their homes on the rack and the wheel.

Though Danton had many and obvious weaknesses he was a good lawyer, and Danton perceived that though he might not have been able to prevent the September massacres, and although they might have been and probably were inevitable under the tension which prevailed, yet that any court, even a political court, would be better than Marat's mob. Some months later he explained his position to the Convention when it was considering the erection of the tribunal which finally sent Danton himself to the scaffold.

"Nothing is more difficult than to define a political crime. But, if a simple citizen, for any ordinary crime, receives immediate punishment, if it is so difficult to reach a political crime, is it not necessary that extraordinary laws . . . intimidate the rebels and reach the culpable? Here public safety requires strong remedies and terrible measures. I see no compromise between ordinary forms and a revolutionary tribunal. History attests this truth; and since members have dared in this assembly to refer to those bloody days which every good citizen has lamented, I say that, if such a tribunal had then existed, the people who have been so often and so cruelly reproached for them, would never have stained them with blood; I say, and I shall have the assent of all who have watched these movements, that no human power could have checked the outburst of the national vengeance."

In this perversion of the courts lay, as I understand it, the foulest horror of the French Revolution. It was the effect of the rigidity of privilege, a rigidity which found its incarnation in the judiciary. The constitutional decisions of the parliaments under the old régime would alone have made their continuance impossible, but the worst evil was that, after the shell crumbled, the mind within the shell survived, and discredited the whole regular administration of justice. When the National Assembly came to examine grievances it found protests against the judicial system from every corner of France, and it referred these petitions to a committee which reported in August, 1789. Setting aside the centralization and consolidation of the system as being, for us, immaterial, the committee laid down four leading principles of reform. First, purchase of place should be abolished, and judicial office should be recognized as a public trust. Second, judges should be confined to applying, and restrained from interpreting, the law. That is to say, the judges should be forbidden to legislate. Third, the judges should be brought into harmony with public opinion by permitting the people to participate in their appointment. Fourth, the tendency toward rigor in criminal cases, which had become a scandal under the old régime, should be tempered by the introduction of the jury. Bergasse proposed that judicial appointments should be made by the executive from among three candidates selected by the provincial assemblies. After long and very remarkable debates the plan was, in substance, adopted in May, 1790, except that the Assembly decided, by a majority of 503 to 450, that the judges should be elected by the people for a term of six years, without executive interference. In the debate Cazalès represented the conservatives, Mirabeau the liberals. The vote was a test vote and shows how strong the conservatives were in the Assembly up to the reorganization of the Clergy in July, 1790, and the electoral assemblies of the districts, which selected the judges, seem, on the whole, to have been rather more conservative than the Assembly. In the election not a sixth of those who were enfranchised voted for the delegates who, in turn, chose the judges, and these delegates were usually either eminent lawyers themselves, or wealthy merchants, or men of letters. The result was a bench not differing much from an old parliament, and equally incapable of understanding the convulsion about them.

Installed early in 1791, not a year elapsed before these magistrates became as ill at ease as had been those whom they displaced, and in March, 1792, Jean Debry formally demanded their recall, although their terms properly were to expire in 1796. During the summer of 1792 they sank into contempt and, after the massacres, the Legislative Assembly, just before its dissolution, provided for a new constituency for the judicial elections. This they degraded so far that, out of fifty-one magistrates to be chosen in Paris, only twelve were professionally trained. Nor did the new courts inspire respect. After the 10th of August one or two special tribunals were organized to try the Swiss Guard who surrendered in the Palace, and other political offenders, but these proved to be so ineffective that Marat thrust them aside, and substituted for them his gangs of murderers. No true and permanent political court was evolved before Danton had to deal with the treason of Dumouriez, nor was this tribunal perfected before Danton gave way to the Committee of Public Safety, when French revolutionary society became incandescent, through universal attack from without and through insurrection within.

Danton, though an orator and a lawyer, possibly even a statesman, was not competent to cope with an emergency which exacted from a minister administrative genius like that of Carnot. Danton's story may be briefly told. At once after Valmy the Convention established the Republic; on January 21, 1793, Louis was beheaded; and between these two events a new movement had occurred. The Revolutionists felt intuitively that, if they remained shut up at home, with enemies without and traitors within, they would be lost. If the new ideas were sound they would spread, and Valmy had proved to them that those ideas had already weakened the invading armies. Danton declared for the natural boundaries of France, — the Rhine, the Alps, and the ocean, — and the Convention, on January 29, 1793, threw Dumouriez on Holland. This provoked war with England, and then north, south, and east the coalition was complete. It represented at least half a million fighting men. Danton, having no military knowledge or experience, fixed his hopes on Dumouriez. To Danton, Dumouriez was the only man who could save France. On November 6, 1792, Dumouriez defeated the Austrians at Jemmapes; on the 14th, he entered

Brussels, and Belgium lay helpless before him. On the question of the treatment of Belgium, the schism began which ended with his desertion. Dumouriez was a conservative who plotted for a royal restoration under, perhaps, Louis Philippe. The Convention, on the contrary, determined to revolutionize Belgium, as France had been revolutionized, and to this end Cambon proposed to confiscate and sell church land and emit assignats. Danton visited Dumouriez to attempt to pacify him, but found him deeply exasperated. Had Danton been more sagacious he would have been suspicious. Unfortunately for him he left Dumouriez in command. In February, Dumouriez invaded Holland and was repulsed, and he then fell back to Brussels, not strong enough to march to Paris without support, it is true, but probably expecting to be strong enough as soon as the Vendean insurrection came to a head. Doubtless he had relations with the rebels. At all events, on March 10, the insurrection began with the massacre of Machecoul, and on March 12, 1793, Dumouriez wrote a letter to the Convention which was equivalent to a declaration of war. He then tried to corrupt his army, but failed, and on

April 4, 1793, fled to the Austrians. Meanwhile, La Vendée was in flames. To appreciate the situation one must read Carnot's account of the border during these weeks when he alone, probably, averted some grave disaster. For my purpose it suffices to say that the pressure was intense, and that this intense pressure brought forth the Revolutionary Tribunal, or the political court.

On March 10, 1793, the Convention passed a decree constituting a court of five judges and a jury, to be elected by the Convention. To these was joined a public prosecutor. Fouquier-Tinville afterward attained to a sombre fame in this position. Six members of the Convention were to sit as a commission to supervise drawing the indictments, the preparation of evidence, and also to advise the prosecutor. The punishments, under the limitations of the Penal Code and other criminal laws, were to be within the discretion of the court, whose judgments were to be final.[1] Death was accompanied by confiscation of property.

Considering that this was an extraordinary tribunal, working under extreme tension, which

[1] *Histoire du Tribunal Revolutionaire de Paris*, H. Wallon, 1, 57.

tried persons against whom usually the evidence was pretty conclusive, its record for the first six months was not discreditable. Between April 6 and September 21, 1793, it rendered sixty-three sentences of death, thirteen of transportation, and thirty-eight acquittals. The trials were held patiently, testimony was heard, and the juries duly deliberated. Nevertheless the Terror deepened as the stress upon the new-born republic increased. Nothing more awful can be imagined than the ordeal which France endured between the meeting of the Convention in September, 1792, and the completion of the Committee of Public Safety in August, 1793. Hemmed in by enemies, the revolution glowed in Paris like molten lava, while yet it was torn by faction. Conservative opinion was represented by the Girondists, radical opinion by the Mountain, and between the two lay the Plain, or the majority of the Convention, who embodied the social centre of gravity. As this central mass swayed, so did supremacy incline. The movement was as accurate as that of any scientific instrument for registering any strain. Dumouriez's treason in April left the northern frontier open, save for a few fortresses which still held out. When those should fall the enemy could make a junction with the rebels in Vendée. Still the Girondists kept control, and even elected Isnard, the most violent among them, President of the Convention. Then they had the temerity to arrest a member of the Commune of Paris, which was the focus of radicalism. That act precipitated the struggle for survival and with it came the change in equilibrium. On June 2, Paris heard of the revolt of Lyons and of the massacre of the patriots. The same day the Sections invaded the Convention and expelled from their seats in the Tuileries twenty-seven Girondists. The Plain or Centre now leant toward the Mountain, and, on July 10, the Committee of Public Safety, which had been first organized on April 6, 1793, directly after Dumouriez's treason, was reorganized by the adition of men like Saint-Just and Couthon, with Prieur, a lawyer of ability and energy, for President. On July 12, 1793, the Austrians took Condé, and on July 28, Valenciennes; while on July 25, Kleber, starving, surrendered Mayence. Nothing now but their own inertia stood between the allies and La Vendée. Thither indeed Kellermann's men were sent, since they had promised not to serve against the coalition for a year, but even of these a division was surrounded and cut to pieces in the disaster of Torfou. A most ferocious civil war soon raged throughout France. Caen, Bordeaux, Lyons, Marseilles, declared against the Convention. The whole of the northwest was drenched in blood by the Chouans. Sixty departments were in arms. On August 28 the Royalists surrendered Toulon to the English, who blockaded the coasts and supplied the needs of the rebels. About Paris the people were actually starving. On July 27 Robespierre entered the Committee of Safety; Carnot, on August 14. This famous committee was a council of ten forming a pure dictatorship. On August 16, the Convention decreed the *Levée en Masse*.

When Carnot became Minister of War to this dictatorship the Republic had 479,000 demoralized soldiers with the colors, under beaten and discredited commanders. Bouillé had conspired against the States-General, Lafayette against the Legislative Assembly, and Dumouriez against the Convention. One year from that time it had a superb force, 732,000 strong, commanded by

Jourdan and Pichegru, Hoche, Moreau, and Bonaparte. Above all Carnot loved Hoche. Up to Valmy the old regular army, however shaken, had remained as a core. Then it became merged in a mass of volunteers, and these volunteers had to be armed and disciplined and fed and led against the greatest and strongest coalition which the modern world had ever seen. France, under Carnot, became a vast workshop. Its most eminent scientific men taught the people how to gather saltpetre and the government how to manufacture powder and artillery. Horses had to be obtained. Carnot was as reckless of himself as of others. He knew no rest. There was that to be done which had to be done quickly and at any cost; there was that or annihilation.

On October 21, 1794, when the people had gathered in the Champ de Mars to celebrate the Festival of Victories, after the President of the Convention had proclaimed that the Republic had been delivered, Carnot announced what had been accomplished.

France had won twenty-seven victories, of which eight had been pitched battles.

One hundred and twenty lesser combats.

France had killed eighty thousand enemies.

Had taken ninety-one thousand prisoners.

Also one hundred and sixteen places or towns, six after siege.

Two hundred and thirty forts or redoubts.

Three thousand eight hundred cannon.

Seventy thousand muskets.

Ninety flags.

As Benjamin Constant has observed, nothing can change the stupendous fact "that the Convention found the enemy at thirty leagues from Paris, . . . and made peace at thirty leagues from Vienna."

Under the stimulus of a change in enviroment a new type of mind is apt to expand with something of this resistless energy. It did so in the Reformation. It may be said almost invariably to do so, when decay does not supervene, and it now concerns us to consider, in some rough way, what the cost to the sinking class of attempting repression may be, when it miscalculates its power in such an emergency.

I take it to be tolerably clear that, if the French privileged classes had accepted the reforms of Turgot in good faith, and thus had spread the movement of the revolution over a generation, there would have been no civil war and no confiscations, save confiscations of ecclesiastical property. I take it also that there would have been no massacres and no revolutionary tribunals, if France in 1793 had fought foreign enemies alone, as England did in 1688. Even as it was the courts did not grow thoroughly political until the preservation of the new type of mind came to hinge largely on the extermination of the old. Danton's first and relatively benign revolutionary tribunal, established in March, 1793, was reorganized by the Committee of Public Safety in the following autumn, by a series of decrees of which the most celebrated is that of September 17, touching suspected persons. By these decrees the tribunal was enlarged so that, in the words of Danton, every day an aristocratic head might fall. The committee presented a list of judges, and the object of the law was to make the possession of a reactionary mind a capital offence. It is only in extreme exigencies that pure thinking by a single person becomes a crime. Ordinarily, a crime consists of a malicious thought coupled with an overt act, but in periods of high tension, the harboring of any given thought becomes criminal. Usually during civil wars test oaths are tendered to suspected persons to discover their loyalty. For several centuries the Church habitually burnt alive all those who denied the test dogma of transubstantiation, and during the worst spasm of the French Revolution to believe in the principle of monarchy and privilege was made capital with confiscation of property.

The question which the Convention had to meet was how to establish the existence of a criminal mind, when nothing tangible indicated it. The old régime had tortured. To prove heresy the Church also had always used torture. The Revolution proceeded more mildly. It acted on suspicion. The process was simple. The Committee, of whom in this department Robespierre was the chief, made lists of those who were to be condemned. There came to be finally almost a complete absence of forms. No evidence was necessarily heard. The accused, if inconvenient, was not allowed to speak. If there were doubt touching the probability of conviction, pressure was put upon the court. I give one or two examples: Scellier, the senior associate judge of the tribunal, appears to have been a good lawyer and a fairly worthy man. One day in February, 1794, Scellier was at dinner with Robespierre, when Robespierre complained of the delays of the court. Scellier replied that without the observance of forms there could be no safety for the innocent. "Bah!" replied Robespierre, — "you and your forms: wait; soon the Committee will obtain a law which will suppress forms, and then we shall see." Scellier ventured no answer. Such a law was drafted by Couthon and actually passed on 22 Prairial (June 10, 1794), and yet it altered little the methods of Fouquier-Tinville as prosecuting officer. Scellier having complained of this law of Prairial to Saint-Just, Saint-Just replied that if he were to report his words, or that he was flinching, to the Committee, Scellier would be arrested. As arrest was tantamount to sentence of death, Scellier continued his work.

Without reasoning the subject out logically from premise to conclusion, or being, of course, capable of doing so in the mass, Frenchmen had collectively received the intuition that everything must be endured for a strong government, and that whatever obstructed that government must be eliminated. For the process of elimination they used the courts. Under the conditions in which they were placed by the domestic enemy, they had little alternative. If a political party opposed the Dictatorship in the Convention, that party must be broken down; if a man seemed likely to become a rival for the Dictatorship, that man must be removed; all who conspired against the Republic must be destroyed as ruthlessly at home as on the battle-field. The Republic was insolvent, and must have money, as it must have men. If the government needed men, it took them, — all. If it needed money, and a man were rich, it did not hesitate to execute him and confiscate his property. There are very famous examples of all these phenomena strewn through the history of the Terror.

The Girondists were liberals. They always had been liberals; they had never conspired against the Republic; but they were impracticable. The ablest of them, Vergniaud, complained before the Tribunal, that he was being tried for what he thought, not for what he had done. This the government denied, but it was true. Nay, more; he was tried not for positive but for negative opinions, and he was convicted and executed, and his friends were convicted and executed with him, because, had they remained in the Convention, the Dictatorship, through their opposition, would have lost its energy. Also the form of the conviction was shocking in the extreme. The defence of these twenty-one men was, practically, suppressed, and the jury were directed to bring in a verdict of guilty. Still the prosecutions of the Girondists stopped here. When they refrained from obstruction, they were spared.

Danton and his friends may have been, and probably were, whether intentionally or by force of circumstances, a menace to the Dictatorship. Either Robespierre or Danton had to be eliminated. There was not room for both. On April 1, 1793, Danton, Camille Desmoulins, and others were arrested on a warrant signed by such men as Cambacérès, Carnot, and Prieur. Carnot in particular was a soldier of the highest character and genius. He would have signed no such warrant had he not thought the emergency pressing. Nor was the risk small. Danton was so popular and so strong before a jury that the government appears to have distrusted even Fouquier-Tinville, for an order was given, and held in suspense, apparently to Henriot, to arrest the President and the Public Prosecutor of the Revolutionary Tribunal, on the day of Danton's trial.

Under such a stimulant Fouquier did his best, but he felt himself to be beaten. Examining Cambon, Danton broke out: "Do you believe us to be conspirators? Look, he laughs, he don't believe it. Record that he has laughed." Fouquier was at his wits' end. If the next day the jury were asked if they had heard enough, and they answered, "No," there would be an acquittal, and then Fouquier's own head would roll into the basket. Probably there might even be insurrection. Fouquier wrote to the Committee that they must obtain from the Convention a decree silencing the defence. So grave was the crisis felt to be that the decree was unanimously voted. When Fouquier heard that the decree was on its way, he said, with a sigh of relief, — "Faith, we need it." But when it was read, Danton sprung to his feet, raging, declaring that the public cried out treason upon it. The President adjourned the court while the hall resounded with the protests of the defendants and the shouts of the police as they tore the condemned from the benches which they clutched and dragged them through the corridors toward the prison. They emerged no more until they mounted the carts which took them to the scaffold.

Nor was it safe to hesitate if one were attached to this court. Fouquier had a clerk named Paris-Fabricius. Now Paris had been a friend of Danton and took his condemnation to heart. He even declined to sign the judgment, which it was his duty to do. The next day, when he presented himself to Fouquier, Fouquier looked at him sourly, and observed, "We don't want men who reason here; we want business done." The following morning Paris did not appear. His friends were disturbed, but he was not to be found. He had been cast into a secret dungeon in the prison of the Luxembourg.

So, if a man were too rich it might go hard with him. Louis-Philippe-Joseph, Duc d'Orleans, afterward known as Égalité, was one of the most interesting figures among the old nobility. The great-great-great-grandson of Louis XIII, he was a distant cousin of Louis XVI, and ranked as the first noble of France beyond the royal family.

His education had been unfortunate. His father lived with a ballet-dancer, while his mother, the Princess Henriette de Bourbon-Conti, scandalized a society which was not easily shocked. During the Terror the sans-culottes everywhere averred that the Duke was the son of a coachman in the service of the banker Duruet. Doubtless this was false, but the princess had abundant liaisons not much more reputable. Left to himself at sixteen years old, Égalité led a life of extreme profligacy, but he married one of the most beautiful and charming women of the age, whom he succeeded in inspiring with a devoted affection. Born in 1747, his father died in 1785, leaving him, just at the outbreak of the Revolution, the master of enormous wealth, and the father of three sons who adored him. The eldest of these was the future king, Louis-Philippe. The man must have had good in him to have been loved as he was throughout life. He was besides more intelligent touching the Revolution and its meaning than any man approaching him in rank in France. The Duke, when a young man, served with credit in the navy, but after the battle of Ushant, in 1778, where he commanded the blue squadron, he was received with such enthusiasm in Paris, that Marie-Antoinette obtained his dismissal from the service. From this period he withdrew from court and his opposition to the government began. He adopted republican ideas, which he drew from America, and he educated his children as democrats. In 1789 he was elected to the States-General, where he supported the fusion of the orders, and attained to a popularity which, on one occasion, according to Madame de Campan, nearly made the Queen faint from rage and grief. It was from the garden of his palace of the Palais Royal that the column marched on July 14, wearing his colors, the red, white and blue, to storm the Bastille. It seemed that he had only to go on resolutely to thrust the King aside and become the ruler of France. He made no effort to do so. Mirabeau is said to have been disgusted with his lack of ambition. He was charitable also, and spent very large sums of money among the poor of Paris during the years of distress which followed upon the social disorders. The breach with the court, however, became steadily wider, and finally he adhered to the party of Danton and voted for the condemnation of the

King. He sent two of his sons to serve in the army. The elder was still with Dumouriez at the time of his treason. On April 6, 1793, when Dumouriez's treachery had become known, the Assembly ordered the arrest of the whole Bourbon family, and among them the Duke was apprehended and sent to Marseilles.

Thus it appears that whatever complaint his own order may have had against Égalité, the Republic certainly had none. No man could have done more for modern France than he. He abandoned his class, renounced his name, gave his money, sent his sons to the war, and voted for his own relative's death. No one feared him, and yet Robespierre had him brought to Paris and guillotined. His trial was a form. Fouquier admitted that he had been condemned before he left Marseilles. The Duke was, however, very rich and the government needed his money. Every one understood the situation. He was told of the order for his arrest one night when at supper in his palace in Paris with his friend Monsieur de Monville. The Duke, much moved, asked Monville if it were not horrible, after all the sacrifices he had made and all that he had done.

"Yes, horrible," said Monville, coolly, "but what would you have? They have taken from your Highness all they could get, you can be of no further use to them. Therefore, they will do to you, what I do with this lemon" (he was squeezing a lemon on a sole); "now I have all the juice." And he threw the lemon into the fireplace. But yet even then Robespierre was not satisfied. He harbored malice against this fallen man. On the way to the scaffold he ordered the cart, in which the Duke sat, to stop before the Palais Royal, which had been confiscated, in order that the Duke might contemplate his last sacrifice for his country. The Duke showed neither fear nor emotion.

All the world knows the story of the Terror. The long processions of carts carrying victims to the guillotine, these increasing in number until after the Law of Prairial they averaged sixty or seventy a day in Paris alone, while in the provinces there was no end. At Nantes, Carrier could not work fast enough by a court, so he sank boat loads of prisoners in the Loire. The hecatombs sacrificed at Lyons, and the "Red Masses" of Orange, have all been described. The population of Toulon sank from 29,000 to 7,000. All those, in fine, were seized and slain who were suspected of having a mind tinged with caste, or of being traitors to the Republic. And it was the Centre, or the majority of the Convention, who did this, by tacitly permitting it to be done. That is to say, France permitted it because the onslaught of the decaying class made atrocities such as these appear to be a condition of self-preservation. I doubt if, in human history, there be such another and so awful an illustration of the possible effects of conservative errors of judgment.

For France never loved the Terror or the loathsome instruments, such as Fouquier-Tinville, or Carrier, or Billaud-Varennes, or Collot-d'Herbois, or Henriot, or Robespierre, or Couthon, who conducted it. On this point there can, I think, be neither doubt nor question. I have tried to show how the Terror began. It is easy to show how and why it ended. As it began automatically by the stress of foreign and domestic war, so it ended automatically when that stress was relieved. And the most curious aspect of the phenomenon is that it did not end through the application of force, but by common consent, and when it had ended, those who had been used for the bloody work could not be endured, and they too were put to death. The procession of dates is convincing.

When, on July 27, 1793, Robespierre entered the Committee of Public Safety, the fortunes of the Republic were near their nadir, but almost immediately, after Carnot took the War Department on August 14, they began to mend. On October 8, 1793, Lyons surrendered; on December 19, 1793, the English evacuated Toulon; and, on December 23, the insurrection in La Vendée received its death blow at Savenai. There had also been success on the frontiers. Carnot put Hoche in command in the Vosges. On December 23, 1793, Hoche defeated Wurmser at Freschweiller, when the Austrians, abandoning the lines of Wissembourg, fell back across the Rhine. Thus by the end of 1793, save for the great border fortresses of Valenciennes and Condé to the north, which commanded the road from Brussels to Paris, the soil of France had been cleared of the enemy, and something resembling domestic tranquillity had been restored at home. Simultaneously, as the pressure lessened, rifts began to appear in the knot of men who held the Dictatorship in the Republic. Robespierre, Couthon, and Saint-Just coalesced, and gained control of the police, while Billaud-Varennes, Collot-d'Herbois, and, secretly and as far as he dared, Barère, formed an opposition. Not that the latter were more moderate or merciful than Robespierre, but because, in the nature of things, there could be but one Dictator, and it became a question of the survival of the fittest. Carnot took little or no part in active politics. He devoted himself to the war, but he disapproved of the Terror and came to a breach with Saint-Just. Robespierre's power culminated on June 10, 1794, with the passage of the Law of 22 Prairial, which put the life of every Frenchman in his hand, and after which, save for some dozen or two of his most intimate and devoted adherents like Saint-Just, Couthon, Le Bas, Fouquier, Fleuriot the Mayor of Paris, and Henriot, the commander of the national guard, no one felt his head safe on his shoulders. It needed but security on the northern frontier to cause the social centre of gravity to shift and Robespierre to fall, and security came with the campaign of Fleurus.

Jourdan and Pichegru were in command on

the Belgian border, and on June 26, 1794, just sixteen days after the passage of the Law of Prairial, Jourdan won the battle of Fleurus. This battle, though not decisive in itself, led to decisive results. It uncovered Valenciennes and Condé, which were invested, closing the entrance to France. On July 11, Jourdan entered Brussels; on July 16, he won a crushing victory before Louvain and the same day Namur opened its gates. On July 23, Pichegru, driving the English before him, seized Antwerp. No Frenchman could longer doubt that France was delivered, and with that certainty the Terror ended without a blow. Eventually the end must have come, but it came instantly, and, according to the old legend, it came through a man's love for a woman.

John Lambert Tallien, the son of the butler of the Marquis of Bercy, was born in 1769, and received an education through the generosity of the marquis, who noticed his intelligence. He became a journeyman printer, and one day in the studio of Madame Lebrun, dressed in his workman's blouse, he met Thérézia Cabarrus, Marquise de Fontenay, the most seductive woman of her time, and fell in love with her on the instant.

Nothing, apparently, could have been more hopeless or absurd. But the Revolution came. Tallien became prominent, was elected to the Convention, grew to be influential, and in September, 1793, was sent to Bordeaux, as representative of the Chamber, or as proconsul, as they called it. There he, the all-powerful despot, found Thérézia, trying to escape to Spain, in prison, humble, poor, shuddering in the shadow of the guillotine. He saved her; he carried her through Bordeaux in triumph in a car by his side. He took her with him to Paris, and there Robespierre threw her into prison, and accused Tallien of corruption. On June 12 Robespierre denounced him to the Convention, and on June 14, 1794, the Jacobins struck his name from the list of the club. When Fleurus was fought Thérézia lay in La Force, daily expecting death, while Tallien had become the soul of the reactionary party. On the 8 Thermidor (July 26, 1794) Tallien received a dagger wrapped in a note signed by Thérézia, — "To-morrow they kill me. Are you then only a coward?"[1]

On the morrow the great day had come. Saint-Just rose in the Convention to read a report to

[1] "C'est demain qu'on me tue; n'etes-vous donc qu'un lache?"

denounce Billaud, Collot, and Carnot. Tallien would not let him be heard. Billaud followed him. Collot was in the chair. Robespierre mounted the tribune and tried to speak. It was not without reason that Thérézia afterwards said, "This little hand had somewhat to do with overthrowing the guillotine," for Tallien sprang on him, dagger in hand, and, grasping him by the throat, cast him from the tribune, exclaiming, "I have armed myself with a dagger to pierce his heart if the Convention dare not order his accusation." Then rose a great shout from the Centre, "Down with the tyrant, arrest him, accuse him!" From the Centre, which until that day had always silently supported the Robespierrian Dictatorship. Robespierre for the last time tried to speak, but his voice failed him. "It's Danton's blood that chokes him; arrest him, arrest him!" they shouted from the Right. Robespierre dropped exhausted on a bench, then they seized him, and his brother, and Couthon, and Saint-Just, and ordered that the police should take them to prison.

But it was one thing for the Convention to seize Robespierre singly, and within its own hall; it was quite another for it to hold him and send him to the guillotine. The whole physical force of Paris was nominally with Robespierre. The Mayor, Fleuriot, closed the barriers, sounded the tocsin, and forbade any jailer to receive the prisoners; while Henriot, who had already been drinking, mounted a horse and galloped forth to rouse the city. Fleuriot caused Robespierre, Couthon, and Le Bas to be brought to the City Hall. A provisional government was completed. It only remained to disperse the Assembly. Henriot undertook a duty which looked easy. He seems to have collected about twenty guns, which he brought to the Tuileries and trained on the hall of the Convention. The deputies thought all was over. Collot-d'Herbois took the chair, which was directly in range, put on his hat, and calmly said, as Henriot gave the order to fire, "We can at least die at our post." No volley came — the men had mutinied. Then the Convention declared Henriot beyond the protection of the law, and Henriot fled to the City Hall. The Convention chose Barras to command their armed force, but save a few police they had no force. The night was wearing away and Fleuriot had not been able to persuade Robespierre to take any decisive step. Robespierre was, indeed, only a pettifogging attorney. At length he consented to sign an appeal to arms. He had written two letters of his name — "Ro" — when a section of police under Barras reached the City Hall. They were but a handful, but the door was unguarded. They mounted the stairs and as Robespierre finished the "o", one of these men, named Merda, fired on him, breaking his jaw. The stain of blood is still on the paper where Robespierre's head fell. They shot Couthon in the leg, they threw Henriot out of the window into a cesspool below where he wallowed all night, while Le Bas blew out his brains. The next day they brought Robespierre to the Convention, but the Convention refused to receive him. They threw him on a table, where he lay, horrible to be seen, his coat torn down the back, his stockings falling over his heels, his shirt open and soaking with blood, speechless, for his mouth was filled with splinters of his broken jaw. Such was the man who the morning before had been Dictator, and master of all the armies of France. Couthon was in little better plight. Twenty-one in all were condemned on the 10 Thermidor and taken in carts to the guillotine. An awful spectacle. There was Robespierre with his disfigured face, half dead, and Fleuriot, and Saint-Just, and Henriot next to Robespierre, his forehead gashed, his right eye hanging down his cheek, dripping with blood, and drenched with the filth of the sewer in which he had passed the night. Under their feet lay the cripple Couthon, who had been thrown in like a sack. Couthon was paralyzed, and he howled in agony as they wrenched him straight to fasten him to the guillotine. It took a quarter of an hour to finish with him, while the crowd exulted. A hundred thousand people saw the procession and not a voice or a hand was raised in protest. The whole world agreed that the Terror should end. But the oldest of those who suffered on the 10 Thermidor was Couthon, who was thirty-eight, Robespierre was thirty-five, and Saint-Just but twenty-seven.

So closed the Terror with the strain which produced it. It will remain a by-word for all time, and yet, appalling as it may have been, it was the legitimate and the logical result of the opposition made by caste to the advent of equality before the law. Also, the political courts served their purpose. They killed out the archaic mind in France, a mind too rigid to adapt itself to a changing environment. Thereafter no organized opposition could ever be maintained against the new social equilibrium. Modern France went on steadily to a readjustment, on the basis of unification, simplification of administration, and equality before the law, first under the Directory, then under the Consulate, and finally under the Empire. With the Empire the Civil Code was completed, which I take to be the greatest effort at codification of modern times. Certainly it has endured until now. Governments have changed. The Empire has yielded to the Monarchy, the Monarchy to the Republic, the Republic to the Empire again, and that once more to the Republic, but the Code which embodies the principle of equality before the law has remained. Fundamentally the social equilibrium has been stable. And a chief reason of this stability has been the organization of the courts upon rational and conservative principles. During the Terror France had her fill of political tribunals. Since the Terror French judges, under every government, have shunned politics and have devoted themselves to construing impartially the Code. Therefore all parties, and all ranks, and all conditions of men have sustained the courts. In France, as in England, there is no class jealousy touching the control of the judiciary.

CHAPTER VI

INFERENCES

As the universe, which at once creates and destroys life, is a complex of infinitely varying forces, history can never repeat itself. It is vain, therefore, to look in the future for some paraphrase of the past. Yet if society be, as I assume it to be, an organism operating on mechanical principles, we may perhaps, by pondering upon history, learn enough of those principles to enable us to view, more intelligently than we otherwise should, the social phenomena about us. What we call civilization is, I suspect, only, in proportion to its perfection, a more or less thorough social centralization, while centralization, very clearly, is an effect of applied science. Civilization is accordingly nearly synonymous with centralization, and is caused by mechanical discoveries, which are applications of scientific knowledge, like the discovery of how to kindle fire, how to build and sail ships, how to smelt metals, how to prepare explosives, how to make paper and print books, and the like. And we perceive on a little consideration that from the first great and fundamental discovery of how to kindle fire, every advance in applied science has accelerated social movement, until the discovery of steam and electricity in the eighteenth and nineteenth centuries quickened movement as movement had never been quickened before. And this quickening has caused the rise of those vast cities, which are at once our pride and our terror.

Social consolidation is, however, not a simple problem, for social consolidation implies an equivalent capacity for administration. I take it to be an axiom, that perfection in administration must be commensurate to the bulk and momentum of the mass to be administered, otherwise the centrifugal will overcome the centripetal force, and the mass will disintegrate. In other words, civilization would dissolve. It is in dealing with administration, as I apprehend, that civilizations have usually, though not always, broken down, for it has been on administrative difficulties that revolutions have for the most part supervened. Advances in administration seem to presuppose the evolution of new governing classes, since, apparently, no established type of mind can adapt itself to changes in environment, even in slow-moving civilizations, as fast as environments change. Thus a moment arrives when the minds of any given dominant type fail to meet the demands made upon them, and are superseded by a younger type, which in turn is set aside by another still younger, until the limit of the administrative genius of that particular race has been reached. Then disintegration sets in, the social momentum is gradually relaxed, and society sinks back to a level at which it can cohere. To us, however, the most distressing aspect of the situation is, that the social acceleration is progressive in proportion to the activity of the scientific mind which makes mechanical discoveries, and it is, therefore, a triumphant science which produces those ever more rapidly recurring changes in environment to which men must adapt themselves at their peril. As, under the stimulant of modern science, the old types fail to sustain themselves, new types have to be equally rapidly evolved, and the rise of a new governing class is always synonymous with a social revolution and a redistribution of property. The Industrial Revolution began almost precisely a century and a half ago, since when the scientific mind has continually gained in power, and, during that period, on an average of once in two generations, the environment has so far shifted that a social revolution has occurred, accompanied by the advent of a new favored class, and a readjustment of wealth. I think that a glance at American history will show this estimate to be within the truth. At the same time such rapidity of intellectual mutation is without precedent, and I should suppose that the mental exhaustion incident thereto must be very considerable.

In America, in 1770, a well-defined aristocracy held control. As an effect of the Industrial Revolution upon industry and commerce, the Revolutionary War occurred, the colonial aristocracy misjudged the environment, adhered to Great Britain, were exiled, lost their property, and perished. Immediately after the American Revolution and also as a part of the Industrial Revolution, the cotton gin was invented, and the cotton gin created in the South another aristocracy, the cotton planters, who flourished until

1860. At this point the changing of the environment, caused largely by the railway, brought a pressure upon the slave-owners against which they, also failing to comprehend their situation, rebelled. They were conquered, suffered confiscation of their property, and perished. Furthermore, the rebellion of the aristocracy at the South was caused, or at all events was accompanied by, the rise of a new dominant class at the North, whose power rested upon the development of steam in transportation and industry. This is the class which has won high fortune by the acceleration of the social movement, and the consequent urban growth of the nineteenth century, and which has now for about two generations dominated in the land. If this class, like its predecessors, has in its turn mistaken its environment, a redistribution of property must occur, distressing, as previous redistributions have been, in proportion to the inflexibility of the sufferers. The last two redistributions have been painful, and, if we examine passing phenomena from this standpoint, they hardly appear to promise much that is reassuring for the future.

Administration is the capacity of coördinating

many, and often conflicting, social energies in a single organism, so adroitly that they shall operate as a unity. This presupposes the power of recognizing a series of relations between numerous special social interests, with all of which no single man can be intimately acquainted. Probably no very highly specialized class can be strong in this intellectual quality because of the intellectual isolation incident to specialization; and yet administration or generalization is not only the faculty upon which social stability rests, but is, possibly, the highest faculty of the human mind. It is precisely in this preëminent requisite for success in government that I suspect the modern capitalistic class to be weak. The scope of the human intellect is necessarily limited, and modern capitalists appear to have been evolved under the stress of an environment which demanded excessive specialization in the direction of a genius adapted to money-making under highly complex industrial conditions. To this money-making attribute all else has been sacrificed, and the modern capitalist not only thinks in terms of money, but he thinks in terms of money more exclusively than the French aristocrat or lawyer ever thought in terms of caste. The modern capitalist looks upon life as a financial combat of a very specialized kind, regulated by a code which he understands and has indeed himself concocted, but which is recognized by no one else in the world. He conceives sovereign powers to be for sale. He may, he thinks, buy them; and if he buys them; he may use them as he pleases. He believes, for instance, that it is the lawful, nay more! in America, that it is the constitutional right of the citizen to buy the national highways, and, having bought them, to use them as a common carrier might use a horse and cart upon a public road. He may sell his service to whom he pleases at what price may suit him, and if by doing so he ruins men and cities, it is nothing to him. He is not responsible, for he is not a trustee for the public. If he be restrained by legislation, that legislation is in his eye an oppression and an outrage, to be annulled or eluded by any means which will not lead to the penitentiary. He knows nothing and cares less, for the relation which highways always have held, and always must hold, to every civilized population, and if he be asked to inform himself on such subjects he resents the suggestion as an insult. He is too specialized to comprehend a social relation, even a fundamental one like this, beyond the narrow circle of his private interests. He might, had he so chosen, have evolved a system of governmental railway regulation, and have administered the system personally, or by his own agents, but he could never be brought to see the advantage to himself of rational concession to obtain a resultant of forces. He resisted all restraint, especially national restraint, believing that his one weapon — money — would be more effective in obtaining what he wanted in state legislatures than in Congress. Thus, of necessity, he precipitates a conflict, instead of establishing an adjustment. He is, therefore, in essence, a revolutionist without being aware of it. The same specialized thinking appears in his reasoning touching actual government. New York City will serve as an illustration.

New York has for two generations been noted for a civic corruption which has been, theoretically, abominable to all good citizens, and which the capitalistic class has denounced as abominable to itself. I suspect this to be an imaginative conception of the situation. Tammany Hall is, I take it, the administrative bureau through which capital purchases its privileges. An incorruptible government would offend capital, because, under such a government, capital would have to obey the law, and privilege would cease. Occasionally, Tammany grows rapacious and exacts too much for its services. Then a reform movement is undertaken, and finally a new management is imposed on Tammany; but when Tammany has consented to a satisfactory scale of prices, the reform ends. To change the system would imply a shift in the seat of power. In fine, money is the weapon of the capitalist as the sword was the weapon of the mediæval soldier; only, as the capitalist is more highly specialized than the soldier ever was, he is more helpless when his single weapon fails him. From the days of William the Conqueror to our own, the great soldier has been, very commonly, a famous statesman also, but I do not now remember, in English or American history, a single capitalist who has earned eminence for comprehensive statesmanship. On the contrary, although many have participated in public affairs, have held high office, and have shown ability therein, capitalists have not unusually, however unjustly, been suspected of having ulterior objects in view, unconnected with the public welfare, such as tariffs or land grants. Certainly, so far as I am aware, no capitalist has ever acquired such influence over his contemporaries as has been attained with apparent ease by men like Cromwell, Washington, or even Jackson.

And this leads, advancing in an orderly manner step by step, to what is, perhaps, to me, the most curious and interesting of all modern intellectual phenomena connected with the specialized mind, — the attitude of the capitalist toward the law. Naturally the capitalist, of all men, might be supposed to be he who would respect and uphold the law most, considering that he is at once the wealthiest and most vulnerable of human beings, when called upon to defend himself by physical force. How defenceless and how incompetent he is in such exigencies, he proved to the world some years ago when he plunged himself and the country into the great Pennsylvania coal strike, with absolutely no preparation. Nevertheless, in spite of his vulnerability, he is of all citizens the most lawless.[1] He appears to assume that the law will always be enforced, when he has need of it, by some special personnel whose duty lies that way, while he may evade the law, when convenient, or bring it into contempt, with impunity. The capitalist seems incapable of feeling his responsibility, as a member of the governing class, in this respect, and that he is bound to uphold the law, no matter what the law may be, in order that others may do the like. If the capitalist has bought some sovereign function, and wishes to abuse it for his own behoof, he regards the law which restrains him as a despotic invasion of his constitutional rights, because, with his specialized mind, he cannot grasp the relation of a sovereign function to the nation as a whole. He, therefore, looks upon the evasion of a law devised for public protection, but inimical to him, as innocent or even meritorious.

If an election be lost, and the legislature, which has been chosen by the majority, cannot be

[1] In these observations on the intellectual tendencies of capital I speak generally. Not only individual capitalists, but great corporations, exist, who are noble examples of law-abiding and intelligent citizenship. Their rarity, however, and their conspicuousness, seem to prove the general rule.

pacified by money, but passes some act which promises to be annoying, the first instinct of the capitalist is to retain counsel, not to advise him touching his duty under the law, but to devise a method by which he may elude it, or, if he cannot elude it, by which he may have it annulled as unconstitutional by the courts. The lawyer who succeeds in this branch of practice is certain to win the highest prizes at the bar. And as capital has had now, for more than one or even two generations, all the prizes of the law within its gift, this attitude of capital has had a profound effect upon shaping the American legal mind. The capitalist, as I infer, regards the constitutional form of government which exists in the United States, as a convenient method of obtaining his own way against a majority, but the lawyer has learned to worship it as a fetich. Nor is this astonishing, for, were written constitutions suppressed, he would lose most of his importance and much of his income. Quite honestly, therefore, the American lawyer has come to believe that a sheet of paper soiled with printers' ink and interpreted by half-a-dozen elderly gentlemen snugly dozing in armchairs, has some inherent and marvellous virtue by which it can arrest the march of omnipotent Nature. And capital gladly accepts this view of American civilization, since hitherto capitalists have usually been able to select the magistrates who decide their causes, perhaps directly through the intervention of some president or governor whom they have had nominated by a convention controlled by their money, or else, if the judiciary has been elective, they have caused sympathetic judges to be chosen by means of a mechanism like Tammany, which they have frankly bought.

I wish to make myself clearly understood. Neither capitalists nor lawyers are necessarily, or even probably, other than conscientious men. What they do is to think with specialized minds. All dominant types have been more or less specialized, if none so much as this, and this specialization has caused, as I understand it, that obtuseness of perception which has been their ruin when the environment which favored them has changed. All that is remarkable about the modern capitalist is the excess of his excentricity, or his deviation from that resultant of forces to which he must conform. To us, however, at present, neither the morality nor the present mental excentricity of the capitalist is so material as the possibility of his acquiring flexibility under pressure, for it would seem to be almost mathematically demonstrable that he will, in the near future, be subjected to a pressure under which he must develop flexibility or be eliminated.

There can be no doubt that the modern environment is changing faster than any environment ever previously changed; therefore, the social centre of gravity constantly tends to shift more rapidly; and therefore, modern civilization has unprecedented need of the administrative or generalizing mind. But, as the mass and momentum of modern society is prodigious, it will require a correspondingly prodigious energy to carry it safely from an unstable to a stable equilibrium. The essential is to generate the energy which brings success; and the more the mind dwells upon the peculiarities of the modern capitalistic class, the more doubts obtrude themselves touching their ability to make the effort, even at present, and still more so to make it in the future as the magnitude of the social organism grows.

One source of capitalistic weakness comes from a lack of proper instruments wherewith to work, even supposing the will of capital to be good; and this lack of administrative ability is somewhat due to the capitalistic attitude toward education. In the United States capital has long owned the leading universities by right of purchase, as it has owned the highways, the currency, and the press, and capital has used the universities, in a general way, to develop capitalistic ideas. This, however, is of no great moment. What is of moment is that capital has commercialized education. Apparently modern society, if it is to cohere, must have a high order of generalizing mind, — a mind which can grasp a multitude of complex relations, — but this is a mind which can, at best, only be produced in small quantity and at high cost. Capital has preferred the specialized mind and that not of the highest quality, since it has found it profitable to set quantity before quality to the limit which the market will endure. Capitalists have never insisted upon raising an educational standard save in science and mechanics, and the relative overstimulation of the scientific mind has now become an actual menace to order because of the inferiority of the administrative intelligence.

Yet, even supposing the synthetic mind of the highest power to be increasing in proportion to the population, instead of, as I suspect, pretty rapidly decreasing, and supposing the capitalist to be fully alive to the need of administrative improvements, a phalanx of Washingtons would be impotent to raise the administrative level of the United States materially, as long as the courts remain censors of legislation; because the province of the censorial court is to dislocate any comprehensive body of legislation, whose effect would be to change the social status. That was the fundamental purpose which underlay the adoption of a written constitution whose object was to keep local sovereignties intact, especially at the South. Jefferson insisted that each sovereignty should by means of nullification protect itself. It was a long step in advance when the nation conquered the prerogative of asserting its own sovereign power through the Supreme Court. Now the intervention of the courts in legislation has become, by the change in environment, as fatal to administration as would have been, in

1800, the success of nullification. I find it difficult to believe that capital, with its specialized views of what constitutes its advantages, its duties, and its responsibilities, and stimulated by a bar moulded to meet its prejudices and requirements, will ever voluntarily assent to the consolidation of the United States to the point at which the interference of the courts with legislation might be eliminated; because, as I have pointed out, capital finds the judicial veto useful as a means of at least temporarily evading the law, while the bar, taken as a whole, quite honestly believes that the universe will obey the judicial decree. No delusion could be profounder and none, perhaps, more dangerous. Courts, I need hardly say, cannot control nature, though by trying to do so they may, like the Parliament of Paris, create a friction which shall induce an appalling catastrophe.

True judicial courts, whether in times of peace or of revolution, seldom fail to be a substantial protection to the weak, because they enforce an established *corpus juris* and conduct trials by recognized forms. It is startling to compare the percentage of convictions to prosecutions, for the same class of offences, in the regular criminal courts during the French Revolution, with the percentage in the Revolutionary Tribunal. And once a stable social equilibrium is reached, all men tend to support judicial courts, if judicial courts exist, from an instinct of self-preservation. This has been amply shown by French experience, and it is here that French history is so illuminating to the American mind. Before the Revolution France had semi-political courts which conduced to the overthrow of Turgot, and, therefore, wrought for violence; but more than this, France, under the old régime, had evolved a legal profession of a cast of mind incompatible with an equal administration of the law. The French courts were, therefore, when trouble came, supported only by a faction, and were cast aside. With that the old régime fell.

The young Duke of Chartres, the son of Égalité Orleans, and the future Louis Philippe, has related in his journal an anecdote which illustrates that subtle poison of distrust which undermines all legal authority, the moment that suspicion of political partiality in the judiciary enters the popular mind. In June, 1791, the Duke went down from Paris to Vendôme to join the regiment of dragoons of which he had been commissioned colonel. One day, soon after he joined, a messenger came to him in haste to tell him that a mob had gathered near by who were about to hang two priests. "I ran thither at once," wrote the Duke; "I spoke to those who seemed most excited and impressed upon them how horrible it was to hang men without trial; besides, to act as hangmen was to enter a trade which they all thought infamous; that they had judges, and that this was their affair. They answered that their judges were aristocrats, and that they did not punish the guilty." That is to say, although the priests were non-jurors, and, therefore, criminals in the eye of the law, the courts would not enforce the law because of political bias.[1] "It is your fault," I said to them, "since you elected them [the judges], but that is no reason why you should do justice yourselves."

Danton explained in the Convention that it was because of the deep distrust of the judiciary

[1] By the Law of November 27, 1790, priests refusing to swear allegiance to the "civil constitution" of the clergy were punished by loss of pay and of rights of citizenship if they continued their functions. By Law of August 26, 1792, by transportation to Cayenne.

in the public mind, which this anecdote shows, that the September massacres occurred, and it was because all republicans knew that the state and the army were full of traitors like Dumouriez, whom the ordinary courts would not punish, that Danton brought forward his bill to organize a true political tribunal to deal with them summarily. When Danton carried through this statute he supposed himself to be at the apex of power and popularity, and to be safe, if any man in France were safe. Very shortly he learned the error in his calculation. Billaud was a member of the Committee of Public Safety, while Danton had allowed himself to be dropped from membership. Danton had just been married, and to an aristocratic wife, and the turmoil of office had grown to be distasteful to him. On March 30, 1794, Billaud somewhat casually remarked, "We must kill Danton;" for in truth Danton, with conservative leanings, was becoming a grave danger to the extreme Jacobins. Had he lived a few months longer he would have been a Thermidorist. Billaud, therefore, only expressed the prevailing Jacobin opinion; so the Jacobins arrested Danton, Camille Desmoulins, and his other friends, and Danton at once anticipated what would be his doom. As he entered his cell he said to his jailer: "I erected the Tribunal. I ask pardon of God and men." But even yet he did not grasp the full meaning of what he had done. At his trial he wished to introduce his evidence fully, protesting "that he should understand the Tribunal since he created it;" nevertheless, he did not understand the Tribunal, he still regarded it as more or less a court. Topino-Lebrun, the artist, did understand it. Topino sat on the jury which tried Danton, and observed that the heart of one of his colleagues seemed failing him. Topino took the waverer aside, and said: "This is not a *trial*, it is a *measure*. Two men are impossible; one must perish. Will you kill Robespierre? — No. — Then by that admission you condemn Danton." Lebrun in these few words went to the root of the matter, and stated the identical principle which underlies our whole doctrine of the Police Power. A political court is not properly a court at all, but an administrative board whose function is to work the will of the dominant faction for the time being. Thus a political court becomes the most formidable of all engines for the destruction of its creators the instant the social equilibrium shifts. So Danton found, in the spring of 1794, when the equilibrium shifted; and so Robespierre, who slew Danton, found the next July, when the equilibrium shifted again.

Danton died on the 5th April, 1794; about three months later Jourdan won the Fleurus campaign. Straightway Thermidor followed, and the Tribunal worked as well for the party of Thermidor as it had for the Jacobins. Carrier, who had wallowed in blood at Nantes, as the ideal Jacobin, walked behind the cart which carried Robespierre to the scaffold, shouting, "Down with the tyrant;" but that did not save him. In vain he protested to the Convention that, were he guilty, the whole Convention was guilty, "down to the President's bell." By a vote of 498 out of 500, Carrier was sent before the Tribunal which, even though reorganized, condemned him. Thérézia Cabarrus gaily presided at the closing of the Jacobin Club, Tallien moved over to the benches on the right, and therefore the court was ruthless to Fouquier. On the 11 Thermidor, seventy members, officers, or partisans of the Commune of Paris, were sent to the guillotine in only two batches. On the next day twelve more followed, four of whom were jurymen. Fouquier's turn came later. It may also be worth while for Americans to observe that a political court is quite as effective against property as against life. The Duke of Orleans is only the most celebrated example of a host of Frenchmen who perished, not because of revenge, fear, or jealousy, but because the party in power wanted their property. The famous Law touching Suspected Persons (loi des suspects) was passed on September 17, 1793. On October 10, 1793, that is three weeks afterward, Saint-Just moved that additional powers should be granted, by the Convention, to the Committee of Public Safety, defining, by way of justification for his motion, those who fell within the purview of this law. Among these, first of all, came "the rich," who by that fact alone were to be considered, *prima facie*, enemies to their country.

As I stated at the beginning of this chapter, history never can repeat itself; therefore, whatever else may happen in the United States, we certainly shall have no Revolutionary Tribunal like the French Tribunal of 1793, but the mechanical principle of the political court always remains the same; it is an administrative board the control of which is useful, or may be even essential, to the success of a dominant faction, and the instinctive comprehension which the American people have of this truth is demonstrated by the determination with which they have, for many years, sought to impose the will of the majority upon the judiciary. Other means failing to meet their expectations, they have now hit on the recall, which is as revolutionary in essence as were the methods used during the Terror. Courts, from the Supreme Court downward, if purged by recall, or a process tantamount to recall, would, under proper stress, work as surely for a required purpose as did the tribunal supervised by Fouquier-Tinville.

These considerations rather lead me to infer that the extreme complexity of the administrative problems presented by modern industrial civilization is beyond the compass of the capitalistic mind. If this be so, American society, as at present organized, with capitalists for the dominant class, can concentrate no further, and, as nothing in the universe is at rest, if it does not concentrate, it must, probably, begin to disintegrate. Indeed we may perceive incipient signs of disintegration all about us. We see, for example, an universal contempt for law, incarnated in the capitalistic class itself, which is responsible for order, and in spite of the awful danger which impends over every rich and physically helpless type should the coercive power collapse. We see it even more distinctly in the chronic war between capital and labor, which government is admittedly unable to control; we see it in the slough of urban politics, inseparable from capitalistic methods of maintaining its ascendancy; and, perhaps, most disquieting of all, we see it in the dissolution of the family which has, for untold ages, been the seat of discipline and the foundation of authority. For the dissolution of the family is peculiarly a phenomenon of our industrial age, and it is caused by the demand of industry for the cheap labor of women and children. Napoleon told the lawyers who drafted the Code that he insisted on one thing alone. They must fortify the family, for, said he, if the family is responsible to the father and the father to me, I can keep order in France. One of the difficulties, therefore, which capital has to meet, by the aid of such administrative ability as it can command, is how to keep order when society no longer rests on the cohesive family, but on highly volatilized individuals as incohesive as grains of sand.

Meditating upon these matters, it is hard to resist the persuasion that unless capital can, in the immediate future, generate an intellectual energy, beyond the sphere of its specialized calling, very much in excess of any intellectual energy of which it has hitherto given promise, and unless it can besides rise to an appreciation of diverse social conditions, as well as to a level of political sagacity, far higher than it has attained within recent years, its relative power in the community must decline. If this be so the symptoms which indicate social disintegration will intensify. As they intensify, the ability of industrial capital to withstand the attacks made upon it will lessen, and this process must go on until capital abandons the contest to defend itself as too costly. Then nothing remains but flight. Under what conditions industrial capital would find migration from America possible, must remain for us beyond the bounds even of speculation. It might escape with little or no loss. On the other hand, it might fare as hardly as did the southern slaveholders. No man can foresee his fate. In the event of adverse fortune, however, the position of capitalists would hardly be improved by the existence of political courts serving a malevolent majority. Whatever may be in store for us, here at least we reach an intelligible conclusion. Should Nature follow such a course as I have suggested, she will settle all our present perplexities as simply and as drastically as she is apt to settle human perturbations, and she will follow logically in the infinitely extended line of her own most impressive precedents.

INDEX

Adams, John: appoints Marshall Chief Justice, 53–61; sent Ellsworth to France, 61; offered office to Jay; chose Marshall, 61.

Adams, John Quincy: extract from diary of, 68.

Administration: inefficiency of, in twentieth century, 3–4; relation to mass, 204; definition of, 207 *et seq.*; lack of ability in, 217; need for, in modern society, 217, 218.

Alien and Sedition Acts: 59.

American Revolution: a revolt against Monopoly, 25; begins with Boston Tea-party, 25.

Arbitration: compulsory, 29, 30; strong government needed for, 29, 30.

Aristocracy: See *Ruling Class.*

Artois, Comte d': emigrates, 146; authorized to organize an army, 148.

Assignats: issued, 149; Cambon wishes to emit in Belgium, 174.

Bastille: stormed, 145.

Bench: See *Judiciary,* and *Courts.*

Billaud-Varenne: an Instrument of the Terror, 191; quarrels with Robespierre, 194; leads Revolution of Thermidor, 197; wants to kill Danton, 222.

Bouillé: commands Army of the North, 146; executes soldiers, 147; tortures soldiers, 155.

Bradley, Mr. Justice: opinion of, in Chicago, Milwaukee and St. Paul Railway *vs.* Minnesota, 102, 103; failed to sustain equality before the law, 115.

Brass vs. North Dakota: 108.

Brunswick, Duke of: manifesto of, 155; threatens reprisals, 156; retreat of, from Valmy, 164.

Burke, Edmund: publishes *Reflections,* and quarrels with Fox, 152; Caste incarnated in, 152.

Cabarrus, Thérézia, Marquise de Fontenay: meets Tallien, 195; adventures of, 196; imprisoned in La Force, 196; sends Tallien a dagger, 196; closes Jacobin Club, 224.

Capitalistic Class: have assumed sovereign powers in America, 13 *et seq.*; irresponsible, 14, 17; have levied taxes, 15; have regulated the currency, 17 *et seq.*; have controlled prices, 25 *et seq.*; supported Washington, 28; now responsible for structure of American Society, 28 *et seq.*; have failed as politicians, 31 *et seq.*; must accept consequences of failure, 32 *et seq.*; probably incapable of appreciating failure, 33; prevail with Supreme Court in Income Tax Case, 74; deflected Supreme Court from its fundamental principle, 98 *et seq.*; antagonistic to equality before the law, 107; favored by Supreme Court, 108 *et seq.*; its pressure on Judiciary in favor of Monopoly, 116–125; apparently breaking down, 207; too highly specialized, 208; arbitrary, 209 *et seq.*; governs by money, 210 *et seq.*; inferior as Statesmen and Soldiers, 211–212; attitude toward law, 212 *et seq.*; probably conscientious, 215; owns universities, 217; uses court to elude majority, 219; physically helpless, 227; likely to abandon America, 288-289; see *English Landlords*; see *Ruling Class, French*.

Carnot: action of, at Dumouriez's treason, 175; joins Committee of Public Safety, 178; becomes Minister of War, 178; announces French victory, 179; signs warrant to arrest Danton, 185; character of, 185, success of, as War Minister, 193; breach of, with Saint Just, 194; denounced by Saint Just, 197.

Carrier: drowns prisoners at Nantes, 191; trial of, executed, 224.

Caste: nature of, 135 *et seq.*; French Judiciary, incarnation of, 136; law of, by Parliament of Paris, 142; defeated in National Assembly, 145; European Society divided by, 147 *et seq.*; first duty of nobility to defend, 148; fused, throughout Europe, 152; law of, laid down at Pilnitz, 155; killed out by Revolutionary Tribunal, 200, 201.

Centre: Party of, supported Party of Mountain, 177; supports Robespierre, 192; attacks Robespierre, 197.

Châlons: objective point of Valmy Campaign, 162.

Charles I: execution of, 14.

Charles X: See *Comte d'Ariois*.

Chartres, Duke of: extract from diary of, 221.

Chase: appointed Chief Justice, 54; decides Hepburn *vs.* Griswold, 72.

Chase, Samuel: impeached, 67.

Châteauvieux, Regiment of: punished after mutiny at Nancy, 146, 147; soldiers of, tortured, 155.

Chicago, Milwaukee and St. Paul R. R. vs. *Minnesota:* 103 *et seq.*

Chisholm vs. *Georgia:* 84.

Church: landed ownership of, 149; confiscation of land of, 149; sale of land of, 149; made hostile by confiscation, 150; constitutional reform of, 150; 221.

Clergy: See *Church*.

Coates vs. *Mayor of New York:* 89.

Coblenz: centre of French Emigration, 151.

Code, Civil: established by Empire, 201; impartially enforced, 202.

Collot d'Herbois: quarrels with Robespierre, 194; denounced by Saint-Just, 197; presides in Convention on Thermidor, 198.

Committee of Public Safety: organized, 177; reorganized, 178; Robespierre and Carnot join, 178; discord in, 194; powers of, enlarged, 225.

Commons; House of: landlords' supremacy over, 133, 134; reform of, 134, 135. See *Parliament*.

Comstock, Mr. Justice: in Wynehamer vs. the People, 95.

Condé, Prince de: 154.

Congress: judicial interference with, 68-79.

Constitution: supported by Washington, 7; crisis when adopted, 8, 9; an imperfect protection, 45; judicial interpretation of, in America, 44, 45; only in America interpreted by judiciary, 47; controversy between Jefferson and Hamilton touching, 49-53; inoperative to restrain Congress, 75-79, 111; made inflexible by judicial decision, 83; altered by judicial legislation, 89; according to Jefferson, wax in hands of judiciary, 127; fetich to lawyers, 214, 219. See *Police Power*.

Convention: meets directly after Valmy, 173; establishes Republic, 173; organizes Revolutionary Tribunal, 175; Girondists expelled from, 177; declares *levée en masse*, 178; reorganizes Committee of Public Safety, 177; reorganizes Tribunal, 181; passes law of Prairial, 183; supports dictatorship of Robespierre, 184 *et seq.*; stops Danton's defence, 186; Revolution of Thermidor, 196-198.

INDEX 233

Corvée: Parliamentary decision touching, 106; nature of, 140; Edict touching, 140; Edict of, rejected by Parliament, 142.

Courts, American: obstruct Mr. Roosevelt, 4; have assumed political power; See *Courts, Political;* have sustained Capital, 16; unsuited to decide political questions, 78; unable to bar encroachments on American Constitution, 75, 111; a bar to administrative reforms, 218; have become a menace to order, 219; tending to become administrative boards, 226; unlikely to be a protection to Capital, 229. See *Courts* below.

Courts, French: Parliament of Paris, the essence of privilege, offices in, vendible, 136, 141; refuses to register Turgot's edict touching *corvée*, 141; defines law of caste, 142; torture regularly used by, 154; old judicial system reorganized by National Assembly, 169 *et seq.;* reorganization inevitable since old courts were semi-political, 169 *et seq.;* pure political courts organized by Danton, 175 *et seq.;* reorganized, 181; see *Revolutionary Tribunal, Danton,* and *Fouquier-Tinville;* Modern French courts, organized under Empire, have been stable because non-political, 201; while old French courts had political bias, and therefore abolished, 220; the revolutionary criminal courts were administrative boards, 223. See *Political Courts*.

Courts, Judicial: definition of, 76; relation of, to Legislature, 76; should administer a code of abstract principles, 81 *et seq.;* this function impossible in America, 81, 82, 83; essentially conservative in contrast to legislatures, 106; should never discriminate, 106, 107; legislation by, destroys, 113; duty of, to protect civil rights, 114, 115; English and modern French Courts true judicial Courts, 114, 129, 130, 201, 202; a defence to the weak, 219.

Courts, Political: Roosevelt's attacks on, 4; in America, 34; effective administration with, impossible, 34; Kings of Israel, political judges, 37; David and Uriah the Hittite, 38 *et seq.;* English political courts, 40 *et seq.;* Jeffreys, C. J., 41 *et seq.;* American and foreign courts, 45; interference with legislation makes courts political, 47; political parties have tried to control American courts, 48 *et seq.;* political controversies touching, in America, 50 *et seq*, 54; Kentucky Resolutions, 59, 60; Marbury *vs.* Madison, 63 *et seq.;* Impeachment of Chase, 67 *et seq.;* Dred Scott Case, 70; Hepburn *vs.* Griswold, 71 *et seq.;* Income Tax Case, 74; Distinction between municipal and political law, 81 *et seq.;* Police Power, a political function, 89 *et seq.;* see *Police Power;* system tends to create active judicial legislation, 124, 125; Trans-Missouri and Standard Oil Cases, 116 *et seq.;* Judicial political functions, lead to elective judiciary and recall, 128; old French judiciary political, 141 *et seq.;* Danton's Revolutionary Tribunal a political court, 168 *et seq.;* see *Revolutionary Tribunal;* in France political courts ceased with the Terror, 200, 201; in France political courts existed prior to Revolution, 220; for that cause abolished, 220; Danton's explanation of, in Revolution, 221, 222; Danton condemned by, 222, 223; are administrative boards, 223; no protection to Capital, 229.

Courts, Roman: 112, 113. See *Praetor*.

Court, Supreme: partisan, 54, 57; arbitrator between Nation and States, 58, 59, 62; **Marbury *vs.***

Madison, 63 *et seq.;* attack on and impeachment of Chase, 67; Missouri Compromise, 70; Hepburn *vs.* Griswold, 71; Knox *vs.* Lee, 73; Income Tax Case, 74; reorganized by slave-owners, 77; constructive, under Marshall, 77; failure of, to control Congress, 78; Jay, Chief Justice of, 84; Chisholm *vs.* Georgia, 84; Marshall, Chief Justice, 85; Dartmouth College Case, 87 *et seq.;* Charles River Bridge Case, 91; construction of Police Power by, 96 *et seq.;* subject to financial influences, 97; follows path of least resistance, 97; Censor of State legislation, 99; rate regulation by, 100 *et seq.;* defines police power, 105; tends to discriminate, 107; Brass *vs.* N. Dakota, 108; Smith *vs.* Ames, 109 *et seq.;* failed to enforce equality before the law because political, 115; exposition of Sherman Act by, 116 *et seq.;* White, Chief Justice, in Standard Oil Case, 119 *et seq.;* at first aided Centralization, 218; likely to become an administrative board, 226. See *Fourteenth Amendment,* and *Dred Scott Case.*

Couthon: drafted law of Prairial, 183; hateful to France, 192; gains control of police, adherent of Robespierre, 194; imprisoned on Thermidor, 197; liberated and reached City Hall, 198; wounded, 199; executed, 200.

Damiens: execution of, 155. See *Torture.*
Danton: a conservative and a lawyer, 153; counsels audacity, becomes Minister of Justice, 159; first heard of Vendée plot, 163; coalesces with Marat, 166; responsibility for September massacres, 166 *et seq.;* defines political crimes, 169; claimed natural boundaries of France, 173; provoked war with England, 173; sustained Dumouriez, 173; reorganizes Tribunal, 181; arrested, 185; convicted, 186; advocates Tribunal, 222; trial of, 223; condemnation of, 223.
Dartmouth College Case: 87.
David, King of Israel: 37 *et seq.*
Disraeli, Benjamin: opinion of Wellington, 134.
Dred Scott Case: 70, 77, 78, 107.
Dumouriez: an adventurer and conservative, succeeds Lafayette in command, 153; wins Jemmapes, 173; trusted by Danton, 173; plots restoration, 174 *et seq.;* invades Holland, 174; treason of, 174, 175.

Ellsworth, Oliver: appointed Chief Justice, 61; sent Envoy to France, 61; resigns, 61.
Emigrants, French: emigration begins, 146; mental condition of, 151; plans of, 151; threats of, 154 *et seq.;* confidence of, 158; sufferings after Valmy, 164 *et seq.*
Environment: effect of, 231, consolidation, result of, 204, 205; revolutions, follow changes in, 180, 206; changes in, rapid in proportion to advances in science, 206 *et seq.;* changes in America inimical to political courts, 218 *et seq.;* modern, is too complex for the predominance of the present capitalistic type, 226 *et seq.*

Financiers: See *Capitalistic Class.*
Fletcher vs. *Peck:* 86.
Fleuriot: mayor of Paris, 194; supported Robespierre in Thermidor, 198; executed, 200.
Fleurus: Campaign of, 195, 196, 224.
Fouquier-Tinville: made prosecuting officer of Tribunal, 175; prosecutes Danton, 185; asked Convention to silence Danton, 186; imprisons Paris-Fabricius, 187; condemned, 224.
Fourteenth Amendment: broadens jurisdiction of Supreme Court,

INDEX

96; effect of, 99 et seq.; Standard Oil Case under, 126.
France: old régime in, 136 et seq.; Privilege in, 138; condition of in 1793, 139. See *Courts, French; Emigrants; Revolution; Revolutionary Tribunal.*
Francis II: comes to throne, 152.

George III: reactionist, 152.
Giles, William Branch: Conversation of, 68.
Girondists: expelled from Assembly, 177; executed, 184, 185.
Grant, U. S., General: reverses Hepburn vs. Griswold, 71.
Guilds: monopolies, 22; regulation of, by Parliament, 22; destroyed by invention of artillery, 23.

Hamilton, Alex.: defence of Constitution, 5; distrusts constitutional limitations, 44, 45; theories of American sovereignty, 49–55; his controversy with Jefferson touching constitutional limitations, 49–53; defines judicial will and judgment, 52, 96, 101; theory of, touching liability of sovereign, 80, 81.
Harlan, Mr. Justice: in Standard Oil Case, 122 et seq.
Henriot: ordered to arrest Fouquier, 186; friend of Robespierre, 194; his action on 10 Thermidor, 198; executed, 200.
Hepburn vs. *Griswold:* 71–73, 124.
Highways: an attribute of Sovereignty, 14; administration of by Romans, 15; by France, 15; views of capitalists touching, 209.
Hoar, Samuel B.: interferes in Hepburn vs. Griswold, 71–73.
Hoche: preferred by Carnot, 179; defeats Austrians, 193.
Holmes, Mr. Justice: defines Police Power, 105, 106.
House of Lords: highest English tribunal, 114; as court, political influences excluded from, 114; fall of, 129 et seq.; remains highest court of appeal, 130.

Huskisson, Wm.: breach with Wellington, 134.

Interstate Commerce Law: 3.

Jackson, General: appointed Taney Chief Justice, 54; successful politician, 212.
Jay, John: appointed Chief Justice, 53; legal theories of, 80; in "Chisholm vs. Georgia," 84; declines Chief Justiceship in 1800, 85; failed to sustain equality before the law, 115.
Jemmapes: Dumouriez wins battle of, 173.
Jeffreys, Chief Justice: 41, 43.
Jefferson, Thomas: dislikes judicial interpretation of Constitution, 48; controversy with Hamilton on it, 48, 49, 50, 51; controversy with Marshall, 59; nullification, 60; Kentucky resolutions, 60; controversy touching Marbury vs. Madison, 63–66; impeaches Chase, 67; declares Constitution to be wax in hands of judiciary, 127; insisted on nullification, 218.
Jourdain: Carnot puts in command, 179; campaign of Fleurus, 195.
Judicial Function: considered, Chap. II, 36; severed from executive function, 40, 43; judicial will and judgment defined, 52; cannot be mingled with politics, 127, 219 et seq. See *Courts* and *Revolutionary Tribunal.*
Judiciary: subserviency of, 44; subjected to pressure because of constitution, 45, 47; censorship of legislatures confined to America, 47; political, 53, 54; political must be partisan, 53–57; distinction between courts and legislatures, 76; exposed to pressure, 82; elective in New York, 128; recall of, 129; status of old French, 136 et seq.; modern French abstains from politics, 201; tends to become tool of majority when invested with

political power, 226. See *Courts* and *Revolutionary Tribunal*.

Kellermann: wins victory of Valmy, 159.
Kentucky Resolutions: 60.
Knox vs. *Lee:* 73.

Labor: a monopoly, 27; war on capital, 28; coercive arbitration of, 30; government unable to control, 227.
Lafayette: a conservative, 153; tried to save the king in 1792, 153; laughed at by Court, 153; Queen refused to be saved by, 154; betrayed by Court, 157.
Landlords, English: hold seats in House of Commons as incorporeal hereditaments, 87, 88; rise of, 133; control of House of Commons, 133; fall of, 135.
Law: relative development of, in eighteenth and twentieth centuries, 11, 12; Washington's problem touching, simple, 12; twentieth century insufficient for modern purposes, 12, 13; equality before, 30, 82; Roman, flexible, 83; Prætor's function, 83; codification of, 112 *et seq.*; equality before, under written constitution, 115; of Caste, 142, 152, 155; tortures under, 154, 182; see *Torture*; combination to suppress equality before, in French Revolution, 161; reformed by National Assembly, 170 *et seq.*; of Prairial, 183; equality before, established in modern France, 201; attitude of capitalists toward, 212 *et seq.*; of Jacobins toward "suspected persons," 225; Saint-Just denounces "the rich" under, 225.
Lawyers: Roman, superiority of, 112; ability of, in the age of Washington, 115; attitude toward Constitution, 214; selected by Capitalistic Class, 214; reverence Constitution, 219; French, 220.

Legislatures: the antithesis of courts, 76; dispensations to, granted by courts under Police Power, 89; cannot be trustworthy court, 113. See *Police Power*.
Leopold II: conference at Pilnitz, 149; restraining influence on Marie Antoinette, 152; death of, 152.
Lincoln, Abraham: appointed Chase Chief Justice, 54.
Louis XVI: attends banquet at Versailles, 146; carried to Paris, 146; captive in Tuileries, 146; plots escape to Metz, 146; created by Caste, 147 *et seq.*; defends Caste, 148; tries to join Army of Bouillé, 148; captured in Tuileries, 157–158; imprisoned in Temple, 158; Royalist indifference to life of, 161; beheaded, 173.
Louis XVIII: See *Comte de Provence*.

Machecoul: massacres at, 165; insurrection of Vendée begins at, 174.
Mallet du Pan: sent to Duke of Brunswick, 155; helps to draw Manifesto, 156.
Marbury vs. *Madison:* 63–66, 67.
Marie Antoinette: attends banquet at Versailles, 146; carried to Paris, 146; sneers at Mirabeau, 147; created by Caste, 147 *et seq.*; sneered at Lafayette, and refused to be saved by him, 153, 154; sent to Temple, 158; her distrust of her brother-in-law, 161; dislike of the Duke of Orleans, 189.
Marshall, John: appointed Chief Justice, 53, 54, 61; constitutional theories, 57, 58; controversy with Jefferson, 59; character of, 62, 63; decides Marbury *vs.* Madison, 63, 64; constructive genius of, 77; legal theories of, 80; theory touching contracts, 85–88; in Dartmouth College Case, 87; failed to sustain equality before the law, 115.

INDEX

Massacres: of Guards at Versailles, 146; of the Swiss Guard, 157; September, 167 *et seq.*; at Machecoul, 174; of patriots at Lyons, 177; Carrier's massacres at Nantes, 191.

Mirabeau: intrigues with Court, 147; exasperated with Queen, 147; a conservative, 145, 153.

Missouri Compromise; 70, 79.

Monopoly: sovereign powers are a, 13; tendency of government to absorb, 20; trade, 21; regulation of, 21; mediæval, 22; Guilds, 22; regulation of by Parliament, 22; royal grants of, held bad, 23, 24; anti-monopoly litigation, 25; not always formed consciously, 26; automatic result of concentration of capital, 26; of labor 27; causes rate regulation, and judicial supervision, 100 *et seq.*; Trans-Missouri Case, 116; Standard Oil, 119; statute to restrain, 124.

Munn vs. Illinois: 101.

National Assembly: States General declared to be, 145; orders fused in, 145; King dissolves, 145; issues assignats, confiscates Church property, 149; secularizes allegiance of the clergy, 150; reforms law, 170 *et seq.*

Nelson, Senator Knute: report on Sherman Act, 118, 119.

New Jersey vs. Wilson: 86. See *Taxes*.

New York City: politics of, capitalists corrupt, 210 *et seq.* See *Tammany Hall*.

Notables: assembly of, 144.

Orleans, Duke of: called Égalité, history of, 187, 188 *et seq.*; arrested by Robespierre, 190; executed, 191.

Parliament, English: regulates mediæval monopoly, 22; absolute, 51; sole grantor of monopoly, 24; seats in, private property, 87, 88; landlords acquired right to return members of, 133; Wellington opposes reform of, 134; Reform bill passed, 135; right to return members of House of Commons an incorporeal hereditament, 88, 137.

Parliament of Paris: offices in, purchasable, 136; judicial position in heritable, 137; Turgot obtained place in, 140; constitutional power of, 141; opinion of touching Corvée, 142; refused to register laws passed by notables, 144; used torture, 154, 155; discredited, 170; new judiciary resembled, 171; caused friction which contributed to revolution, 219; a semi-political court, 141, 220.

Pichegru: put in command, 179; takes Antwerp, 195.

Pilnitz: meeting at, 149; manifestoes at, 155, 156; royalist commentary on declaration at, in 1791, 161.

Pinckney, Charles: suggests congressional power over State legislation, 56.

Police Power: origination of, theory of, 89; defined, 92, 93, 94, 105; extension of, 96–106; effort at definition of, 98, 105; reasonable exercise of, 98–105, 108, 109 *et seq.*; exercise of in Standard Oil Case, 125; identical with principle underlying Revolutionary Tribunal, 223.

Prætor: Roman, function of, 83.

Prairial: law of, drafted, 183; executions under, 191.

Prices: See *Monopoly*.

Prussia: King of, at Pilnitz, 149; manifesto of, 155, at Valmy, 164.

Railways: highways, 15; public agents, 15; owned by private persons, 16; rates are taxes, 16, 17; Trans-Missouri Case, 116 *et. seq.*

Recall: Mr. Roosevelt's proposition to recall judicial decisions, 4; of judges, an effect of political courts,

129; of judges, a revolutionary measure, 226.

Reform Bill: of 1832, 135.

Revolution, French: caused by intellectual rigidity, 135; condition of France prior to, 136 *et seq.*; judicial system contributed to, 137; unequal taxes contributed to, 138, 139; Turgot attempted to moderate, 140 *et seq.*; destroyed Caste, 143, 201; beginning of, 144, 145; aristocracy failed to understand, 147 *et seq.*; caused emigration of aristocracy, 148; created peasant land-owners, 149, 150; Caste resisted, 152; combination to suppress, 151, 155; won at Valmy, 159; royalist theories concerning, 161; September massacres, 167; considered servile revolt, 168; due to Royalists, 165, 168; reforms law, 170 *et seq.*; coalition against, completed, 173; culminates in 1793, 176; see *Committee of Public Safety*; insurrection against, 178; victories won by, 179, 180; creates a criminal process, 182 *et seq.*; famous trials during, 184 *et seq.*; violent period of, ends with Thermidor, 196; can never be repeated, 203, 225.

Revolution, Industrial: causes fall of English landlords, 133; causes American revolution, 206; causes rise of Southern planters, 206; of industrial capitalists, 207.

Revolutionary Tribunal: organized, 175; executions by, in 1793, 175, 176; reorganized by Danton, 181; defined treason, 181 *et seq.*; intimidated, 182–187; Danton bewailed erection of, 223; an administrative board, 223; always obeyed the majority, 224; condemns the rich, 225; impossible in America, 225, 226.

Revolutions: occur periodically, 6 *et seq.*; caused by advance in applied science, 10; violent revolutions caused by resistance to change, 133; frequent in proportion to changes in environment, 204–208; intellectual exhaustion caused by, proportionate to frequency, 206.

Robespierre: joins Committee of Public Safety, 178; demands suppression of forms in Tribunal, 183; malice toward Duke of Orleans, 191; quarrels with Billaud and Callot, 194; power culminates, 194; denounces Tallien, 196; sends Thérézia to La Force, 196; imprisoned, 198; liberated, 198; wounded on Thermidor, 199; executed, 200.

Roland: would abandon Paris, 158, 159; failed to stop Massacres, 167.

Roosevelt, Theodore: his problem in 1912, 3; difficulties of, in 1912, 4, 5, 6; attitude to centralization, 6; offence against capital, 32.

Rouerie, Marquis de la: goes to Coblenz, 150.

Ruling Class: rigid, 33; in France, nobility, clergy, and lawyers, 142–143; necessarily destroyed, 143, 201; struggle between them and Commons, 145; politically incapable, 147 *et seq.*; emigrants, 148, 151; creatures of Caste, 151 *et seq.*; manifestoes of, 155 *et seq.*; defeated at Valmy, 159; their plan of campaign, 161 *et seq.*; brought on massacres, 165 *et seq.*; error of, touching Revolution, 168; wage civil war in France, 178; exterminated, 201; shifts of, 205.

Saint-Just: denounces Billaud, Collot, and Carnot, 197; executed, 200; denounces rich under law of "suspected persons," 225.

Science, Applied: the cause of Revolution, 10; effect of, in nineteenth century, 11 *et seq.*; effect of applied science on sovereignty, 14; effect on Police, 23; effect on Labor, 27; increases cost of administration, 139; causes social acceleration and disintegration,

203–205; capitalists raise standard of, 217; its predominance, a menace, 217.
Sherman Act: 3; Senate sustains, 118; passed in 1890, 124; Congress may amend, 126; amended by White, C. J., 119, 123–126.
Slaughter-House Cases: 99.
Smith vs. *Ames:* 109.
Sovereignty: Washington's problem touching, 9 *et seq.;* powers of, defined, 13; held as a trust, 13; when held irresponsibly, termed slavery, 14; absorbed in United States by private persons, 15 *et seq.;* sovereignty is a concentration of energy, 19 *et seq.;* a true monopoly, 20–24; capital as sovereign, 29; capitalistic sovereignty must be strong, 29–34; relation of courts to, 34; political courts, instruments of despotic, 37–44; Jefferson's theory touching usurpation of, by American courts, 52, 127; State sovereignty, 80–81; courts usurp under Police Power, 91 *et seq.;* American now hinges on Police Power, 105; see *Police Power;* cannot be limited by courts, 111 *et seq.;* French sovereignty passes to National Assembly, 145; caste sovereignty, fall of, 148 *et seq.;* see *Caste;* absorbed by Committee of Public Safety, 178; see *Committee of Public Safety; Revolution, French;* and *Revolutionary Tribunal;* capitalist, conceives sovereign powers to be for sale, 209; capitalistic notion of sovereign functions, 213 *et seq.;* sovereignty of U. S. once asserted through Supreme Court, 218; Supreme Court now disintegrates sovereignty, 218, 219; administrative sovereignty cannot be exercised through true courts, 223, 224; see *Political Courts;* modern capitalists apparently unable to hold their sovereignty, 226 *et seq.*
Standard Oil Case: 119 *et seq.*

States General: summoned, 144. See *National Assembly.*
Story, Joseph: extract from opinion of, in Charles River Bridge Case, 8; view in Charles River Bridge Case, 90, 91.
Tallien: sketch of, 195; fell in love with Thérézia Cabarrus, 195; elected to Convention, 196; saves Thérézia, 196; attacks Robespierre, 197; joined party of the Right, 224.
Tammany Hall: capitalistic engine, 211; used to nominate judges, 215.
Taney: Chief Justice, appointed by Jackson, 54; in Dred Scott Case, 70; in Charles River Bridge Case, 91.
Terror: how caused, 176 *et seq.;* how ended, 192 *et seq.;* loathed by France, 192; instruments of, put to death, 193; end of, 195, 200. See *French Revolution* and *Committee of Public Safety.*
Thermidor, Tenth of: Saint-Just tries to denounce Billaud, Collot, and Carnot, 196–197; attack on Robespierre and Saint-Just, 197; successful, 198 *et seq.;* executions on eleventh of, 224, 225.
Torture: used as means of punishment in army, 147, 155; an integral part of the old French law, 154; public torture habitual, torture of Damiens, 154, 155; French emigrants believed that they could intimidate the revolutionary army by threats of, 151, 154, 155; threatened by them and by the Duke of Brunswick, 156, 157; used by the insurgents at Machecoul in Vendée, 165; a scandal under the old régime and suppressed by Revolution, 170, 182; Church for ages habitually tortured, and so did French courts, 182.
Toulon: surrendered to English, 178; decrease in population of, 191; evacuated, 193.

Trans-Missouri Case: 116 et seq.; rule in, approved by Congress, 118; overruled by White, C. J., 119 et seq.

Tuileries: stormed August 10th, 157; plan for defence of, 157, 162.

Turgot, Robert: history of, 139 et seq.; edict touching Corvée, 140; breach with Parliament, 141; predicts insolvency of France, 143.

Uriah, the Hittite: Case of, 38.

U. S. Steel Co.: management of, 29.

Valmy: victory of, 159, 161 et seq.

Vendée, La: cause of insurrection in, 150; begins in, 165, 174; massacre at Machecoul, 165; defeat of insurrection in, 193.

Vergniaud: trial of, 184. See *Girondists*.

War Power: 97.

Washington, General: reform of Confederation by, 7; his solution of problems presented by Confederation, 9, 10; his advantage as a reformer in eighteenth century, 11; eighteenth century law sufficed for, 12, 13; appoints John Jay Chief Justice, 53; appoints Ellsworth Chief Justice, 61.

Wellington, Duke of: in the reform agitation, 134, 135; Disraeli's opinion of, 134, 135.

White, Edward Douglas: Chief Justice, in Income Tax Case, 74; in Standard Oil Case, 119, 120 et seq.

THE following pages contain advertisements of Macmillan books by the same author and on kindred subjects.

By BROOKS ADAMS

The Law of Civilization and Decay

AN ESSAY ON HISTORY

Cloth, 8vo, $2.00 net

"The author has a simple and strong manner of stating facts and drawing conclusions, and his fascinating style makes the book not only readable, but very entertaining." — *Home Journal.*

"It is particularly brilliant in its generalization concerning the modern employments of the race energy that once made war a profession and a necessity." — *Lincoln Evening News.*

"The book is very suggestive; it presents a theory of history which must be reckoned with; and is remarkable for the skill with which the facts are selected." — *American Historical Review.*

The New Empire

Cloth, 12mo, $1.50 net

"A work of great dignity and erudition, showing rare familiarity with the data of history, theology, and economics." — *Philadelphia Evening Bulletin.*

"The argument is interesting and stimulating. . . . The book is well written and worth reading, and those who have any interest whatever in historical subjects should not overlook it." — *Providence Journal.*

THE MACMILLAN COMPANY

Publishers   **64-66 Fifth Avenue**   **New York**

By SCOTT NEARING, Ph.D.
Of the Wharton School, University of Pennsylvania

Social Adjustment

Cloth, 377 pages, $1.50 net

"It is a good book, and will help any one interested in the study of present social problems." — *Christian Standard.*

"A clear, sane gathering together of the sociological dicta of to-day. Its range is wide — education, wages, distribution and housing of population, conditions of women, home decadence, tenure of working life and causes of distress, child labor, unemployment, and remedial methods. A capital reading book for the million, a text-book for church and school, and a companion for the economist of the study desk." — *Book News Monthly.*

Wages in the United States

Cloth, 12mo, $1.25 net; postpaid, $1.35

This work represents an examination of statistics offered by various states and industries in an effort to determine the average wage in the United States. As a scholarly and yet simple statement it is a valuable contribution to the study of one side of our social organization.

The Law of the Employment of Labor

By L. D. CLARK

Cloth, 12mo, $1.60 net

In all the realm of economics it is strange that heretofore no book has been published dealing specifically and authoritatively with the legal aspects of labor. Mr. Clark has realized this, and his book covers the whole field of law as it affects the employment of labor in the United States. By the citation of an adequate number of representative cases and statutes, the principles of common law in their most important phases as well as the nature and trend of legislation are discussed and illustrated in so far as these are applicable to workmen and their employers.

THE MACMILLAN COMPANY

Publishers   64-66 Fifth Avenue   **New York**

By EDWARD A. ROSS

Professor of Sociology, University of Wisconsin
Formerly of the University of Nebraska

Social Psychology

Cloth, 8vo, $1.50 net

"The volume marks off for itself a very definite field of research, and scours the circumscribed area in the most scientific manner. . . . Professor Ross has laid bare the more vital social traits, good and bad, of the human mind in a manner calculated to awaken thought." — *The New York Tribune.*

Social Control

A Survey of the Foundations of Order

PART I — THE GROUNDS OF CONTROL
PART II — THE MEANS OF CONTROL
PART III — THE SYSTEM OF CONTROL

Cloth, 12mo, leather back, $1.25 net

The author seeks to determine how far the order we see about us is due to influences that reach men and women from without, that is, social influences. His thesis is that the personality freely unfolding under conditions of healthy fellowship may arrive at a goodness all its own, and that order is explained partly by this tendency in human nature and partly by the influence of social surroundings. The author's task, therefore, is first to separate the individual's contribution to social order from that of society, and second, to bring to light everything that is contained in this social contribution.

Foundations of Sociology

The Scope and Task of Sociology — The Sociological Frontier of Economics — Social Laws — The Unit of Investigation in Sociology — Mobmind — The Properties of Group-Units — The Social Forces — The Factors of Social Change — Recent Tendencies in Sociology — The Causes of Race Superiority — The Value Rank of the American People.

The author lays a foundation for a social science that shall withstand the severest tests, and formulates the principal truths about society. In the belief that the time is past for one-sided interpretations of society, the effort is made to group together and harmonize the valuable results of all the schools.

Both the above are in "The Citizen's Library" of Economics, Politics, and Sociology, edited by RICHARD T. ELY, Ph.D., LL.D., Professor of Political Economy, University of Wisconsin.

THE MACMILLAN COMPANY

Publishers   **64-66 Fifth Avenue**   **New York**

American Social Progress Series

EDITED BY

PROFESSOR SAMUEL McCUNE LINDSAY, PH.D., LL.D.,

COLUMBIA UNIVERSITY

A series of handbooks for the student and general reader, giving the results of the newer social thought and of recent scientific investigations of the facts of American social life and institutions. Each volume about 200 pages.

1 — **The New Basis of Civilization.** By SIMON N. PATTEN, Ph.D., LL.D., University of Pennsylvania. *Price*, $1.00 *net*.

2 — **Standards of Public Morality.** By ARTHUR TWINING HADLEY, Ph.D., LL.D., President of Yale University. *Price*, $1.00 *net*.

3 — **Misery and Its Causes.** By EDWARD T. DEVINE, Ph.D., LL.D., Columbia University. *Price*, $1.25 *net*.

4 — **Government Action for Social Welfare.** By JEREMIAH W. JENKS, Ph.D., LL.D., Cornell University. *Price*, $1.00 *net*.

5 — **Social Insurance.** A Program of Social Reform. By HENRY ROGERS SEAGER, Ph.D., Columbia University. *Price*, $1.00 *net*.

6 — **The Social Basis of Religion.** By SIMON N. PATTEN, Ph.D., LL.D., University of Pennsylvania. *Price*, $1.25 *net*.

7 — **Social Reform and the Constitution.** By FRANK J. GOODNOW, LL.D., Columbia University. *Cloth*, 12mo, $1.50 *net*.

THE MACMILLAN COMPANY

Publishers   64–66 Fifth Avenue   New York

The Social Unrest
Studies in Labor and Social Movements

Cloth, 12mo, 394 pages, $1.50 net

By JOHN GRAHAM BROOKS

"Mr. Brooks has given the name of 'Social Unrest' to his profound study, primarily of American conditions, but incidentally of conditions in all the civilized countries. The book is not easy reading, but it would be difficult to find a volume which would better repay thorough digestion than this. It expresses with absolute justice, I think, the conflicting interests. It shows the fallacies of many socialistic ideals. It admits the errors of the unions. It understands the prejudices of the rich and the nature of their fear when present arrangements are threatened. And the sole purpose of the author is to state the truth, without preference, without passion, as it appears to one who has seen much and who cares how his fellowman enjoys and suffers.

"Mr. Brooks does not guess. He has been in the mines, in the factories, knowing the laborers, knowing the employers, through twenty years of investigation." — *Collier's Weekly*.

"The author, Mr. John Graham Brooks, takes up and discusses through nearly four hundred pages the economic significance of the social questions of the hour, the master passions at work among us, men *versus* machinery, and the solution of our present ills in a better concurrence than at present exists — an organization whereby every advantage of cheaper service and cheaper product shall go direct to the whole body of the people. . . . Nothing upon his subject so comprehensive and at the same time popular in treatment as this book has been issued in our country. It is a volume with live knowledge — not only for workman but for capitalist, and the student of the body politic — for every one who lives — and who does not ? — upon the product of labor." — *The Outlook*.

Mr. Bliss Perry, the editor of *The Atlantic Monthly*, says of it: "A fascinating book — to me the clearest, sanest, most helpful discussion of economic and human problems I have read for years."

Mr. Edward Cary, in *New York Times' Saturday Review*, writes: "Hardly a page but bears evidence of his patience, industry, acuteness, and fair-mindedness. . . . We wish it were possible that his book could be very generally read on both sides. Its manifest fairness and sympathy as regards the workingmen will tend to the accomplishment of this result; its equal candor and intelligence with regard to the employers should have a like effect with them."

"Perhaps the most valuable portion of it is that which treats of French and German Socialism, in the knowledge of which the author probably has few superiors in this country." — *Literary Digest*.

THE MACMILLAN COMPANY
Publishers   **64-66 Fifth Avenue**   **New York**